D0866636

99637

BRO DART Printed in U.S.A.

RUTGERS UNIVERSITY STUDIES IN ENGLISH

NUMBER FOUR

LETTERS OF THOMAS HOOD

Letters of
THOMAS HOOD

From the DILKE *papers in the*
BRITISH MUSEUM

Edited with an Introduction and Notes
By LESLIE A. MARCHAND

New Brunswick

RUTGERS UNIVERSITY PRESS

1945

COPYRIGHT 1945 BY THE TRUSTEES OF
RUTGERS COLLEGE IN NEW JERSEY

All Rights Reserved

THIS BOOK IS MANUFACTURED IN ACCORDANCE WITH
ORDERS ISSUED BY THE WAR PRODUCTION BOARD FOR
CONSERVING PAPER AND OTHER VITAL MATERIALS

Printed in the United States of America

To PLEASANT MEMORIES OF ENGLAND AND OF ENGLISH PEO-
PLE: *memories of London streets and country woods and lanes; of the place names that are poetry and history combined; of bus rides to Hampstead Heath and Chingford and Hampton Court; of melody-filled Sunday mornings ringing with the songs of street-singers and the mellow tones of ancient bells; of English breakfasts and Lyons Corner Houses and the domed quiet of the British Museum Reading Room; of the inflections of English speech on the street and in the theatre; of English hospitality and cozy coal fires—to all these and many more nostalgic memories of the country and the compatriots of Thomas Hood I dedicate this little volume of his letters.*

99637

Contents

LETTERS OF THOMAS HOOD

Introduction

IN THE WINTER OF 1935-36, while searching for material which would throw light on my study of the *Athenaeum* and its editor, Charles Wentworth Dilke, I was directed by Miss Gertrude Tuckwell, niece and literary executrix of Sir Charles Dilke (grandson of the editor), to the Manu-script Room of the British Museum where, a short time before, she had sent some letters and other family papers of the Dilkes. Though they were not yet catalogued or even mounted, the Keeper of the Manuscripts and his assistants were kind enough to let me examine these papers and make copies of them at will. Among them was a packet of letters from Thomas Hood to the elder Dilke and to Mrs. Dilke. On the folder enclosing them was written (probably by Sir Charles Dilke): "Six letters. These two long letters of Hood's have never been published—but the published one to Dr. Elliot of the same date [Jan., 1836] contains some of the same points." In the same enclosure was the following letter:

Master's House
   Temple, E. C.
      Dec. 20, 1897
Dear Sir Charles Dilke.
   I am returning herewith all the MSS. letters and frag-ments that you so kindly entrusted to me many years ago. I hope and believe that they are intact, & in as good preservation as when you lent them to me—I ven-ture to wonder whether among the smallest & slightest

fragments you could manage to spare me one, as a valued autograph of Hood—which I do not as yet possess. I hope that you sympathise on the whole with my view of Hood. The Press have been so far very kind to me—in particular Mr. Quiller Couch, in the pages of the *Speaker*.

Once more thanking you for your much kindness
I remain
Yours very truly
Alfred Ainger

Although Canon Ainger had these letters in his possession for several years while he was preparing his two-volume edition of the *Poems of Thomas Hood* (1897), he did not quote a line from them in his introduction, and in fact made only a vague oblique reference to one, that concerning the quarrel of Hood with his wife's family. Ainger was possibly the first and last person outside of the Dilke family to see the letters before Miss Tuckwell sent them to the British Museum.

There were among the Dilke papers in the British Museum, in addition to the six letters already mentioned, several shorter ones, mostly undated, and some fragments of letters, poems, and prose sketches.[1] With a few exceptions, mostly of material already published, these manuscripts are all reproduced here as they were found.[2] The two long letters from Coblenz, written closely in Hood's neat and (for the most part) very legible hand on large foolscap

[1] The catalog number of the Hood papers in the Dilke collection is Add. 43,913.

[2] Items in the collection which are not included here are: three poems published in the *Athenaeum* ("The Fall," "Miss Fanny's Farewell Flowers," and "Reply to Pauper"); a letter of Jan. 19, 1841, declining a present of £50 from the Literary Fund (published in Dilke's *Papers of a Critic*, 1875); and a few incomplete doggerel lines.

folios, were not ordinary communications dashed off to catch the daily post, but extended and leisurely commentaries on the life in Germany which served as trial paragraphs of material which he was later to use in the *Comic Annual* and *Up the Rhine*. The composition of each letter was turned to from day to day over a period of perhaps a fortnight or more. It was an outlet for Hood such as conversation would have been to another man. Like conversation these letters run from comic to serious and reveal the attractive personality of the writer.

Thomas Hood was a prolific letter writer. Perhaps less than half of his correspondence has so far been published. The two-volume *Memorials of Thomas Hood*, "collected, arranged, and edited by his daughter, with a preface and notes by his son," published by Moxon in 1860, contains only part of the family correspondence, a number of long letters to the Dilkes and the Elliots, a few to Dickens, and some miscellaneous ones to various correspondents. It is a disappointing work because of its omissions and also because of its rather haphazard editing. Walter Jerrold's *Thomas Hood: His Life and Times* (1907), the only full length biography, has relied heavily upon the *Memorials*, as was necessary, but has added some letters from the earlier period of Hood's life and a very few from the later.

Less accessible but known to be extant are the many unpublished letters of Hood in libraries in America and in England, and in the hands of dealers and collectors. But in addition to these there must still exist somewhere an even larger, and possibly more interesting, number which are yet unknown and which, if they shall have escaped demolition and incendiary and robot bombs, may one day be discovered and printed. Any attempt to make these letters more available cannot but afford satisfaction to the admirers of Hood, for in the total estimate of his work, his letters are by no means to be neglected.

Whether it would have been advisable to save the few letters and fragments now first published in this volume for inclusion in a larger collection of Hood's correspondence is a subject which might be argued with some reason on both sides. But it has seemed to me that the inherent interest of the letters themselves, the probable inaccessibility of the manuscripts, because of the war, for some years to come, and the light they throw, important though not tremendous, upon the life and character of Hood, are considerations which justify separate publication.

In the main Hood was an entertaining letter writer. He had a journalist's sense of the interest that lies in common things and an effervescent love of fun which was constantly bubbling over in his most casual composition as well as in his published work. Punning was a natural manner of expression for Hood and not necessarily a sign of frivolity; it often crept into his most serious writing. The mixture of the serious and the comic is best to be seen in some of his long letters to his closest friends, where he displayed his personality most unreservedly.

In none of his letters was Hood more at ease, more frank, or more sincere than in those he sent to his friend Charles Wentworth Dilke, whom he had probably met as early as 1821 during his *London Magazine* days, for Dilke had also been a contributor to that brilliant journal in the 1820's.[3] In 1830 when Dilke took control of the *Athenaeum*, a weekly journal of literature, music, drama, fine arts, science, and every interest of the educated or cultured, Hood and

[3] This is the view of Hood's son. Dilke's grandson says, however: "The acquaintance of Mr. Dilke and Mr. Hood dated from 1816, their warm friendship from 1830." *Papers of a Critic* (1875), I, 54.

his brother-in-law, John Hamilton Reynolds, became partners in the venture. They both (Reynolds certainly and Hood probably) withdrew, however, when Dilke in 1831 lowered the price from 8d. to 4d. against their advice. But they probably soon saw their shortsightedness, for the circulation of the magazine increased sixfold in a few days. Nevertheless they both continued to contribute to the *Athenaeum* for a number of years, though Hood's contributions consisted of little more than a few humorous and punning reviews, an occasional poem such as the *Ode to Rae Wilson* (1837), some amusing letters to the editor concerning the *Comic Annual*, and a series of articles on "Copyright and Copywrong" in 1837 and again in 1842.

Although many of his contemporaries thought Dilke austere to a spartan extreme because he shunned the society of literary coteries in an effort to maintain the critical independence of his journal, he nevertheless had a capacity for warm and lasting friendship and a reputation for honesty and soundness of judgment. The words "Consult Dilke" in Hood's first letter to his wife from Coblenz attest to the trust which many of Dilke's intimates, from Keats to Dickens, had in him. Hood's confidence is nowhere more in evidence than in the long feverish letter from Lake House here published for the first time. And in the more intimate portions of Hood's letters from Germany there is further tribute to Dilke's good judgment and friendly understanding. It is true that while Hood, even in times of severe illness and suffering, was always full of irrepressible puns and practical jokes, Dilke was inclined to be ultra-serious if not dogmatic. Keats, though warmly attached to Dilke, had once called him a "Godwin-Methodist," and one "who cannot feel he has a personal identity unless he has made up his Mind about every thing." [4] But, different as Dilke and Hood were, they had a basis of friendship in many views shared in common, especially certain generous enthusiasms, a passion for public morality and social justice, as well as private integrity, and a hatred for cant and hypocrisy. So "the grave editor," as Hood playfully called him, became the warmest friend as well as counsellor of the jester who had a great core of the serious in his nature too. It is not surprising that some of Hood's most revealing letters were written to Dilke.

The story of the relation between Hood and the Reynolds family can be pieced out only from fragmentary evidence. The friendship of Hood and John Hamilton Reynolds began as early as 1821 when they were fellow contributors to the *London Magazine*. Reynolds was four and a half years older and had been a bosom friend of Keats, and he was himself a poet of promise with a flair for satire, his most successful piece being a parody of Wordsworth's "Idiot Boy" manner in a poem which he called "Peter Bell." It was shortly after the publication of *Odes and Addresses to Great People*, a volume of light verse by Hood and Reynolds, that Hood married John's sister, Jane Reynolds (May 5, 1825).

Jane was, as Hood indicated playfully but sincerely in the long letter to Dilke from Coblenz, an ideal wife for a man of Hood's temperament, occupation, and propensity for practical joking. She copied his manuscripts, cared for him tenderly in his illnesses, and had sufficient gullibility and no resentment for his jokes such as that of the trussing of the pudding described in the Coblenz letter. Their mutual understanding was undoubtedly the brightest flame

[4] *Letters of John Keats*, ed. H. Buxton Forman, II, 466.

that lighted the many days of care and pain in Hood's short life.

After the quarrel with the sisters of Jane, the origin of which is indicated pretty clearly in the letter of 1835 in this collection, Hood probably saw less of the Reynolds family, but there are some hints in other letters that the Hoods and the Reynoldses were on terms of friendliness again within a year or two. It is probable that Hood never quarreled seriously with his old friend John Hamilton Reynolds, though he had some disagreements, which, it may well be, arose out of the quarrels with other members of the family as indicated in the letter mentioned above. Certainly, Hood was not the man to hold a permanent grudge. Nevertheless, his biographer says that some months after his death "Jane Hood and John Hamilton Reynolds met and were reconciled at their mother's bedside, after a quarrel of some years' standing, the occasion of which is not known." [5] Apparently the reconciliation did not extend to Reynolds's wife, for Tom Hood the younger says in a footnote to the *Memorials* (1860): "A frequent correspondence was kept up between my father and him [Reynolds], which would have afforded materials of much value toward the compilation of these memorials. I regret to say they are unavailable, owing to Mrs. John Reynolds' refusal to allow us access to them." [6]

Of the other friends of the Hoods mentioned in the letters only a word need be said. The origin and nature of the friendship of the Hoods with Lieutenant Philip De Franck are made sufficiently clear in the letters themselves and in the appended notes. The same may be said for the other acquaintances and friends of the Hoods in Coblenz. Dr.

[5] Jerrold, *op. cit.*, 396.
[6] *Memorials*, I, 11.

William Elliot of Stratford (not Shakespeare's Stratford but the one in the environs of London) was Hood's physician and devoted friend from 1835 until his death in 1845. Though he is mentioned infrequently in these letters, Hood's correspondence with him is, next to that with Dilke, the most frank and cordial. During at least one of Hood's most serious illnesses, when he had hemorrhages of the lungs, Dr. and Mrs. Elliot took him into their own home and gave him the tenderest care.

Hood's whole later life must be viewed against the background of these frequently recurring illnesses, even though he himself made light of them for the most part in his letters. He apparently had his first serious seizure of spasms in the chest in April, 1835, shortly after his arrival in Coblenz, having greatly overdone himself before he left England, and having suffered intense fatigue and strain in a very stormy crossing of the North Sea. He recovered, however, and enjoyed some measure of health until the end of 1836. In a note on his father's trip with Lieutenant De Franck's regiment in September and October of that year, Tom Hood the younger says: "These were almost the last of my father's days of health, and henceforward—although there have been occasional mentions of illness before—the letters will record the gradual but sure decline of it." [7] Indeed, it is surprising that Hood accomplished so much and remained so cheerful in the constant struggle with illness which marked the few remaining years of his life. Dr. Elliot, writing to Mrs. Hood on May 11, 1840, diagnosed the disease as

an enlargement and thickening of it [the heart],—with contraction of the valves, and . . . hemorrhage from

[7] *Memorials*, I, 191.

the lungs, or spitting of blood, recurring very frequently. There is also disorder of the liver and stomach. These diseases have been greatly aggravated of late years by the nature of his pursuits,—by the necessity, which, I understand, has existed, that he should at all times continue his literary labours. . . . The great and continued excitement attendant on such compulsory efforts, the privation of sleep and rest . . . and the consequent anxiety, depression, and exhaustion have had a most injurious effect on these diseases, bringing on renewed attacks. . . .[8]

Specific references in the letters in this volume to Hood's difficulties as author and editor are, I believe, made clear enough in the notes, but the general subject of his relations with his publishers and his quarrels with them has never been completely clarified by his biographers. No available extant letters throw much light on the matter, though something may be pieced together from the rather vague references in the *Memorials* and from other slight evidence in letters published and unpublished. What is certain is that Hood changed publishers several times during his short writing career, and that he felt himself tricked and defrauded by most of them, especially by Charles Tilt and A. H. Baily. He started legal action against Baily about 1840, and the acrimonious battle with him continued through the remainder of Hood's life. His relations with Henry Colburn, proprietor of the *New Monthly Magazine*, were never very happy while Hood edited that journal from 1841 to 1843. Colburn had his own underlings, such as Shoberl (mentioned in some of the letters in this collection), hired independently of the editor to do the puffing of books published by Colburn. Until further evidence is

[8] *Ibid.*, II, 236-237.

produced it is impossible to say whether or how much Hood was to blame in these squabbles with publishers. He was probably impractical and an easy prey to sharp practices of the business world, and his fault may have been nothing more than lack of business sense in choosing his publishers, and lack of care in making agreements with them.

One other matter in Hood's biography has not yet been cleared up, that of the financial embarrassments which he suffered in 1834 and 1835, mentioned in the letter from Coblenz to Dilke in this volume. The statement in the *Memorials* is purposely vague: "At the end of 1834, by the failure of a firm my father suffered, in common with many others, very heavy loss, and consequently became involved in pecuniary difficulties." [9] Richard Garnett adds, on what authority is not known, that Hood's losses "appear to have been due to the failure of a publisher," [10] and Jerrold, probably following Garnett, has said the same.[11] Perhaps some day letters or other documents will turn up which will solve the mystery. In the meantime, the frankness of Hood's account of his reaction to that loss in his long letter to Dilke in this volume will have to satisfy the curious.

Matters other than lacunae in the biography of Hood, however, have somewhat complicated the task of editing this volume. The knowledge that some at least of its limitations and shortcomings are directly or indirectly attributable to the inconveniences of war may increase the indulgence of the reader. In the first place it has been impossible to check my own copy, made more than nine years ago, with the original letters. Even though more than usual care

[9] *Memorials*, I, 49.
[10] *D. N. B.* article on Hood.
[11] Jerrold, *op. cit.*, p. 270.

was exercised in the copying, it is probable, ordinary allowances for human frailty being made, that some errors have crept in. For those I take full responsibility. The best I could do under the circumstances was to follow my own manuscript copy as faithfully as possible. I am confident that my copying errors have not been many or important and that they have not marred an understanding of the matter. I have indicated omissions due to imperfections in the originals, and when a word was not clear in Hood's handwriting, I have sometimes bracketed my own guesses (with a question mark) in order to fill out the text. This has not been frequent. I have had to trust my manuscript for spelling, punctuation, and abbreviations, which (with due allowances for error again) were all copied exactly as they were found in the letters.

An attempt has been made to arrange the longer letters in a chronological sequence, so far as that can be established by dates, postmarks, or internal evidence. The shorter letters and fragments are grouped together after these, and other poetic and prose fragments come at the end. References in the notes to the *Memorials of Thomas Hood* are to the first edition (Moxon, 1860), and those to *Up the Rhine* are to Volume VII of *The Works of Thomas Hood*, edited, with notes, by his son and daughter (London, Ward, Lock & Co., n. d. [1882-1884]).

It had been my wish to pay the customary courtesies to the descendants or heirs of Thomas Hood, if there be any, by asking their permission to publish these letters, but so far my efforts to establish contact with them have been fruitless. The uncertainties of wartime communication being what they are, I am proceeding without further search, hoping that if this volume should ever come to the notice of any such persons concerned they will recognize that it has been published in good faith and with the desire to increase the knowledge of Thomas Hood among those who, having a sympathy for him, are his natural heirs. My thanks are due to Miss Gertrude Tuckwell, who directed me to the Dilke papers in the British Museum, and to the Keeper of the manuscripts and other staff members of the Museum, who permitted me to copy the letters. I am grateful to Mr. Walter M. Teller for the loan of certain Hood materials in his possession, and to Professor George L. Marsh for information concerning the life of John Hamilton Reynolds. And I wish to express my appreciation and thanks to Miss Joyce L. Kellogg for a critical reading of the introduction and notes and for helpful suggestions in matters of arranging and editing.

Letters

["Go Poor Fly—"]

Lake House, Monday Night
7. o'clock
(9th Feby) [1835]

My dear Dilke

Here I sit, solus, in that large drawing-room, with a sick wife upstairs,[1]—a sick child in the next room to this— (Fanny[2] has sickened with the measles)—and a fly-load of company has just departed, containing Mr. & Mrs. Green & Miss Charlotte Reynolds,[3] the two children & nursemaid. As a true Philosopher I have found comforts in the three predicaments—Jane is better, enough to atone for all the rest—but then poor Fanny is ill,—yet hath her illness this relief in it, that it hath hastened away the aforesaid fly with its living lumber,—The Greens, the Charlotte, the two young Greens & their nursemaid, no slight relief to the larder of a man whose poulterer hath today refused a pair of fowls[4]—& those were people who would eat fowls if fowls were to be had. But that is a trifle to the load off my

---

[1] Jane Hood was seriously ill following the birth of Tom Junior, January 19, 1835.

[2] Fanny (Frances Freeling Hood) was about five years old. She was born some time in 1830; the exact date is not known.

[3] Mrs. Green was formerly Marian Reynolds, Jane Hood's sister, and Charlotte was another sister of Jane.

[4] Hood was in financial difficulties and his creditors were pressing him. (See p. 30.)

head. I have had misgivings whether my anxiety for Jane might not make me somewhat rough in my remonstrances, but in a case of such vital interest, a little hardness on my part might have been forgiven—but the manner of their departure reconciles me perfectly to all I have done, so as only to leave a doubt whether I went far enough. Only the old lady [5] remains & if sometimes wrong headed she is always right-hearted, & I am sure forgives me for sometimes opposing the first characteristic. I tried to make all smooth, with Marian, with whom I had gone most smoothly,—before they went—but as she chose to consider herself insulted (i.e. that Green had insulted me,)—I let them go, without seeking or finding a farewell, feeling that such treatment of a man who has devoted himself life, soul and body to their sister's welfare, deserved something better than they could bestow, & had it already, in the recovery of his better self. My last words were, that as they had *given Jane over*, they would forgive me, any offence on my part if I should restore her whole to them—a contemptuous reply sealed my feeling toward them for ever, & I have whistled them down the wind.

No one of them has worked the tithe of what I have—twice have I pitched headlong from my chair with extreme watching,—but still I am in heart & alert for the dear object of my efforts is I hope accomplished, yet what was done to oppress me in my sore time of trouble I cannot forgive or forget—it must be as endurable in my memory as "The Most Terrible Ten Days of my Life." How should I relish the comfort of true friends if I am not to feel & taste the baseness & bitterness of false ones? Green in defending Lotte against me chose to tell me that I had been guilty of

[5] Mrs. Reynolds, Jane Hood's mother.

"disgraceful caballing." I, who stood *alone*—caballing with myself—or with the Doctors—or with my poor Wife—for I had no other confederates! My indignation has settled into deep disgust & we shall never be well again whilst I retain my nature. I can forgive their oblivion of me, the little credit I have obtained for efforts, superhuman, in proportion to my own exhausted strength, having just got through my two books,[6]—though on the personal acct. I could never condescend to admit such on my list of friends —but I cannot forget that thro them or some or all of them my poor girl went thro all but the torments of hell. A curse I say on such selfish ones! Jane never saw *me* shed a tear, or heard a misgiving word till given over,—that true tenderness will be called callousness,—my love to her will be called hate to them,—I know what I am to expect from the style of their departure. My comfort is I have real friends (as yourself) who know me better—& I can appeal to a very domestic life, in proof of my sincere love for Jane, & to unbiassed testimony in favour of my exertions "not to be a widower before my time." It relieves my jaded heart to throw itself thus upon yours,—to requite me for such unworthy treatment.—There—I am better—& they are worse. What a world we live in!—I am quite convinced all my theories of laughter & tears, &c.—are gospel. What think you of a rat hunt in a sick chamber? Yet was it enacted today at Lake House, & Rose killed her rat in style having hunted it under the bed to the fire-place. I believe I shall be an altered man—more of a philosopher—scorning the hollow & enjoying the real in joy or grief. I feel something of the spirit of Lamb when he wrote to me—"We have had all the world (i.e. Green) & his wife here in the last week or two

[6] *Tylney Hall* and the *Comic Annual* for 1835, both published in 1834.

—they seem to have come I know not whence, but they have all gone & have left room for a quiet couple. We are quiet as death, & lonely as his dark chambers. But parting wears off as we shall wear off—the great remedy is to be as merry as we can, & the great secret is how to be so." [7]

Even so with myself,—emerging from the Valley of the Shadow of Death—wherein I have made a progress beset by the fair but false friends. My dear Dilke loves me, as I love you,—or I could not write thus, with a free outpouring of spirit—you must be my ventilator—for I have lately been choked with cursed moral fogs vapours & stinking ignes fatui, bright but rottenness. An hour with you would do me good—but next to that, is this letter, wherein I do most cordially grasp your hand & grapple you into mine heart with hooks of steel. But I am rambling as wildly almost as Jane has lately wandered,—you must allow for the revulsion of feeling that seeks this vent. Times of intense stealthy agony—hours of forced cheerfulness—long nights of earnest watching, of breath & pulse,—myself a very spider as it were on the fine spun web of life—lovings, sorrowings, hopings, despairings—hope sometimes a comet, sometimes a fixed star—sometimes a shooting one, dropping suddenly from the seventh heaven—add every energy of mind concentrated to observe, understand, & discriminate the phenomena of a very nice case,—the internal conflicts, the external skirmishes,—all these & more might be my excuses for a more than usual excitement, now that a favourable result has been obtained, after a storm, during which I had seen every hope but my own driven from its anchor— Oh my God Dilke if ever I fought the good fight of faith, or had any pretentions to a mind it was during this frightful

[7] This letter of Lamb is not in the latest and most complete edition of Lamb's letters edited by E. V. Lucas (1935).

struggle! There was a hope—but it was like a Romeo await-
ing the revival of his Juliet in a dank charnel, of bones
hideous, chokefull,—musicked by a Choir of Ravens. Love,
only, love, could have stood the ordeal & it did. *That* will
be the blessing of my life. Come what may Jane & I henceforth must be dear above dear to each other! It will be as
we had passed the tomb *together* & were walking hand in
hand in Elysium! Out of the fulness of the heart and of the
head I write—but I am dreadfully mistaken, if you do not
understand me in every word—have no fear of my firmness
of mind or self command—this is only a *relief*, which, if
you have had as kind a friend as I write to, you have some-
time or other, I guess, had reason to appreciate. Moreover,
I may be depreciated, misrepresented & in the tenderest
point—and these my feelings will remain upon record in
your hands—you will know, little as I have paraded it elsewhere, that my heart soul & strength have been engaged in
the struggle that has just passed, & that whatever I may
have seemed to the senseless & shallow, my dear Jane was
an object that I have been diving deep after, nigh unto
drowning, in the river of Life. As I sat serene & silent in
the darkest hour, & cheerful in the dreariest, so even now,
with people round me in common converse, my heart is
singing paeans of joy for my Eurydice. It only grieves me
that I cannot yet get her out of the accursed Cavern, of
her Fears—to use her own words she "still smells of earth"—
a shovel-full of earth's dirtiest in the dismal faces that first
planted that cruel terror! She must have suffered terribly—
I read most unutterable things in her face,—& curst the spell
that was laid upon her spirit. Think me not mad, my dear
Dilke, but I am writing of things words cannot reach. Hor-
rors, horrible, most horrible, must have been her portion.
Still, I beg, let this not pass beyond ourselves, but when we

meet I can circumstantially prove to you what I say—namely she was half-killed by fear, & her friends, if so to be called. You may suppose therefore that amongst the other Demons that beset & tormented me, Scorn, Indignation, anger, & I was going to say Hatred were not missing.

I have not written myself calmer for I began calmly—but it is time to talk of calmer things. My best, & dearest, has been composed all day, no rambling, but a doubt how to decide between me (Hope personified,—but a unit) & "her family"—as many Despairs as Members, *here*. I have as it were to clear the mire from her eyes, to take the dust out of her mouth—to restore her from among that marble multitude, in the Arabian Nights. But the sweet end is this—*all other* troubles disappear,—& come poverty, age[?], and all other ills, with my wife & honour and poverty & my two babes, I still will love the world & thank its ruler. And now you know more of T. Hood than you could gather from a Comic Annual, or the whole series, or the Whims,[8] or anything I have ever written, saving this letter,—& you will believe I am happy—tho much moved. This is one of the few outbreaks I have indulged in, thro a trying & variable storm,—& you will excuse it, perhaps thank me, for addressing it to yourself, always kindest to me in trouble, & I have therefore the less remorse in troubling you with my joy. I have not written such a Gog of a letter for years, nor have I gone thro such gigantic feelings. But it has cost me no pains—my pen ran away with me—or rather my heart with my pen. The light of my hearth is not extinguished— & I delight in the fresh blaze up of the old fuel of love.

[8] The *Comic Annual*, written and illustrated with wood blocks by Hood, began in 1830 and continued through 1839. *Whims and Oddities*, first series, was published in 1826; the second series appeared in 1827.

May my domestic agonies avert yours—a little while since I scarcely thought again to enjoy your fire side or my own. I am perhaps writing weakly, foolishly,—but it is because I have nothing to do. When called upon I was not wanting—but a heavenly rest has arrived—a calm after a storm, & thro the clearing up rack I see *Home!*—still *Home!* A word that had almost slipped out of the dictionary of my life. I have still a wife—a comfort I would have poor J. H. R.[9] hug to his heart as I do—poor fellow, I pitied him in the midst of my own seeming calamity,—for I thought of my next Star of Magnitude, my own Fanny.[10] Curse Halley's Comet! It is high unpropitious. I have not a friend whose star shines as it ought. It will gratify you both to know that Jane mentioned you both repeatedly in her delirium even—for the heart looks after the head in its wanderings, like a mother after a stray child. In hot days men open their windows, in the warmth of passion & feeling so we open our hearts to give the soul a breathing—thus you see into mine. I am becoming Coleridgean Kantean, high metaphysical,—but common-place suits not my present mood. There is much of positive & negative moral electricity to work off & I make you one of my conductors. God bless you,—I feel to-night a Rothschild who might have been a beggar, supposing one's purse of wealth carried somewhere about the left breast pocket. But I have learned to know the true metal from the base,—no Marian flash notes, no Lotte smashing, none of Green's flimsies for me. As they have voluntarily left my house, without *farewell*, they must not look for Welcome, which is its Irish Echo,—they are gone with Bad

[9] John Hamilton Reynolds, Jane Hood's brother. (See Introduction, pp. 7-8.)
[10] Reynolds had just lost his only child, a daughter ten years of age.

Taste & Bad Feeling for their companions & black and bad be the day, that sees them over my threshold. If I love *her*—if I respect myself so it must be. *Locke* says know thyself, —and unto you my dear Dilke I entrust the *key* to what may be the future conduct of

Yours in confidence & in true &
everlasting friendship.
Thos. Hood.

I do not say burn this letter, but preserve it. Have no fears for me,—for till we meet, herein I bury my feelings. I ought to give you some news however, if only for the sake of Mrs. Dilke, whose kindness, like yours, I know by intuition. My views in life are changed—& would have been whether Jane lived or died, as you know, & I shall want your advice & will draw upon it at once, without scruple. [*Should I be unfortunate I will drop you, for you well* (this crossed out as italicized)] But I am changed. In some things my eyes are opened & my heart is shut. I disdain hypocrisy. Toward Jane I must feel more devoutly loving than on that dear day that made me her husband,—she has given me proofs of her love, from the tomb, & beyond the tomb,—I am as sure of her heart as if I now held her in heaven. But the same dreadful security that sealed that bond, hath shown me where I *am not* loved & no hollow professions in the world shall make me prostitute a holy passion of benevolence & goodwill, by bestowing my friendship even on the hollow & heartless. I have accompanied my Jane to the brink of the grave, & some stood there to see her into it—& when she was rescued from it, they did not joy as I do. I will not curse them—but the veriest *stranger who never knew her* hath more share in my regard than they have. Selah, as the Psalm says—for it is getting like a psalm. My eyes have been widely opened—to the present, the past, & the future. My beloved seemed to see visions & so did I in reality. I know my position. Should it ever be said,—as it may, & I think will be said—that I was no devoted husband, these pages will be in proof. My life will be in better proof,—with the best opportunities, if cultivated, of moving in the best society, I have sought my domestic joys. My friends in general will do me justice tho I should be in disfavour with a few. I do not mean to submit to Little Britain [11] Leading Strings,—my Jane is ten times dearer to me for this trial, but some others have blotted themselves even from my Black Book,—they will be to me, as they had never been.

I take fright at the length of this letter, but my feelings write twenty such a day. It is a comfort to me. It is a scorn, a loathing, to me to see petty spites, & passions, congregating around death beds, which are but the stepping-blocks to heaven. Good God that the presence of Death himself cannot control our most paltry passions! They pretend to love my wife, & yet but for me, & the very measures they hate me for, she would have been a victim! The next wife I have next to death's door, the next relation that comes next her, with a hope next to nothing and a face to match, shall enjoy the next common.

This is a *great big* letter already—so I need not bid you *make much of it*. I have never before written such a one, & may never again. But I can never again have such cause. So treasure it. It is a record of the present feelings at least of one you know & may prove an illustration of permanent opinions. I will not go further—Jane, tonight (Monday

[11] A street in the old city of London near Aldersgate where the Reynoldses lived.

12 a/m) is better & improving,—would we could all say as much.

Believe me

Dear Dilke

Yours very truly,

Thos. Hood.

I mean what I write. The *realities* of life have come so home to me that I will not put up with its humbugs. This is henceforth the motto of yours ever.

T. H.—

Another morning—and Jane is better. She may now be thought out of danger. I took a whole sleep last night for the first time,—& did not dream. If I had it would have been of Jane trying to swim in the River of Life with sisterly Millstones round her neck,—or to fly in the vital air, with a deep-sea lead to each leg, like those encumbered pigeons of St. Mark,—I mean those turned out from the Basilica on Palm Sunday at Venice, with weights tied to their legs. I shall love Clark's fly forever—the man who drove and the horses that drew it. Sweetly did it diminish in the distance, & lose itself thro that gate at Can Hall Lane. Then did I feel with Shandy—"Go poor fly—there is room in the world for thee and me." [12] There is no magic nowadays—or had I known a formula for transforming that one horse vehicle into the Andromeda, or the Amphitrite, bound anywhere,— say New South Wales,—God forgive me, but I fear I should have pronounced it on the spot! What could be their sports

[12] See *Tristram Shandy*, Vol. II, Chap. 12. Punning was such a habit with Hood that it crept into his serious as well as his humorous writing.

when children? Did they dramatize De Foe's History of the plague & go about with a tiny go cart & bell & a cry of bring out your dead! I shall never believe in hearts,—they have but two of those stone wins [wens?] in their bosoms, as funereal & unfeeling. In strict justice & consistency, [ought?] not such death-doing thoughts & feelings to turn homeward,—making them suicidal,—filo [*sic*] de se—ought not one to take laudanum or deadly nightshade & hellebore, & the other to drown herself in the blackest pool that can be found search[?] England thorough—some pond in a cut-throat lane, with water as still as death & as black as a coffin, from running thro the sable mud of the Slough of Despond. Or is the despairing feeling only a show—an affectation,—born of a damnd pride—disdaining to have been mistaken, —and resenting the idea of being outgone in firmness, common sense, age & good feeling for the sufferer, by such a thing as a sister's husband—a brother-in-law! The male sex stand not on a high pedestal in L. B. [Little Britain] Fathers —Brothers—& so forth are but hewers of wood & drawers of water,—domestic spaniels to fetch & carry—& verily that Green is the pet lapdog of the house, with an ignoble collar round his neck to show to whom he belongs. He looks tame & fat. You are right about fools—give me the Knaves, with crooked heads,—they have sometimes hearts. But who can bear a fellow with a head like a cocoanut & a heart like a walnut's. As my gate closed behind them, I felt a corresponding slam in my bosom—they are shut out & for ever. This is not written in anger, under the fever of irritation, but after rest & sleep—with a steady hand & a cool head,— between them & me there is henceforth a great gulf fixed,— impassable whilst memory endures—even that dreary Inferno of Dante into which they would have dragged my Beatrice—bless her! This is bitter writing but treacled words cannot flow from a pen that drips in a cup of gall, forced upon me. I have had a revelation like St. John's, by the light of the star Wormwood, when "the third part of the waters became wormwood & many men died of the waters because they were made bitter."

I am not mad most noble Dilke but speak the words of truth & soberness.—It is no splenetic misanthropic mood against all the world. Warmly I feel to you or I could not write thus—& sweet, intensely sweet, is my little Goshen, as it were widened by this narrowing. Sweet it is to have been able to pay off a dividend of that tender care, nursing & devotion I owe of old to my most excellent Jane. There are harsh chords which will jar if touched upon, but there are others that discourse most excellent music, & those mute melodies are now singing in my soul, lulling many worldly cares to sleep. Have no care for me. My mind which has stood firm throughout will not fail me *now*. But there are times in a man's life when his thoughts become intensified, so as to review a past life & project a future in a few short hours. Such has been my case. Jane's illness will be a marked aera to me,—& will have much influence on what is to come. The exigency of the time has called forth a decision I knew not belonged to me, & I mean to cherish it. It has been a great comfort to me to think & know that I have true friends who will feel with and for me,—who will appreciate my motives & give me credit for right feeling, & consequent right conduct, in the most critical & trying crisis of my life. I know that J. H. R. was told otherwise, but I sent him yesterday a copy of the following; which I send for your satisfaction—it is from Dr. Elliot. I merely asked him to certify as to Jane, in order to contradict the sinister reports they persisted in spreading.

My dear Sir.

I am quite delighted to observe so much amendment in Mrs. Hood even since last evening. There is now fair prospect of her complaint going off smoothly. And you have kept up your courage surprisingly under the severe and tedious trial. Your health seems not to have suffered at all.

Yours mo truly

9th Feby.

W. Elliot.

My health did suffer tho for awhile from incessant watching, which if I remitted, every good was undone again. But I kept that to myself—& fought myself well again—on Sunday I was threatened with a fit—my mouth was convulsed—& no wonder. I cannot describe my torments I will say atrociously inflicted. *The cup was full enough before.* I have just heard that Lotte (the worst) was to return here today. If so my mind is made up to tell her she shall not stay—I will not have my all endangered at the 11th hour. What think you of such infernal sentiments as follow. When the Dr. had said Jane was in a good sleep—the best thing for her—Lotte said *to me* "I hope she will wake sensible, & then pass away quietly."—And Wright [13] heard her say "What gave her horror was, that if Jane had been let alone she would have died days ago!" Damn such pestential sensibility—Does she want a dead sister to cry over, let her give her good wishes to Marian.

The Dr. has arrived & I will give you his report ere I close. He says she is as well as yesterday, the head, &c. well,—but some disorder of the bowels has supervened which requires care. I have just seen her—she is quite col-

[13] Hood's friend John Wright of the firm of Wright and Folkard, wood engravers of Fenchurch Street, later handled most of the business pertaining to the publication of the *Comic Annual* while Hood was abroad.

lected, & conscious of the past, that there has been a struggle between me and the rest. I have had it from her own lips. And now haven't I been well beset—to say nothing of annoyances, signed, sealed, & delivered,—but which I do not feel *now*. God bless you and yours & keep your roof from all such visitations. [corner torn out of last sheet—signature or what?]

[Englishman on the Rhine]

372 Castor Hof Coblenz "Prosit Neujahr!"
[Jan., 1836]

My dear Dilke

The letters came at last—on the last day of the year! Some of them dated October the fourteenth! It was an expressive silence enough but we did not muse your praise. Sometimes we thought all England must have drowned itself—sometimes we doubted we were only at Coblenz & fancied ourselves like Elia's Distant Correspondents, on those shores where "haunts the Kangaroo." There seemed a *spell* against those letters & with me I fear it occasionally spelt d-a-m-n. To be sure twas provoking to Christian patience to see that infernal orange band & orange collar go so often to the very next door. The *eil*wagen [1] seemed turned to winegar. First Jane fumed,—and then I did,—for which I got lectured, Madam being comparatively cool, from having fumed herself out. By way of climax, think of Mrs. L. [2] being detained nearly a fortnight with our letters at Rotterdam, because somebody in England had neglected

[1] *Eilwagen* (express wagon or fast coach, which apparently carried the mail) forced into a pun on eil (oil?) turned to vinegar?
[2] Unidentified.

28

to ship [her?] luggage. In the meantime, as dumness [*sic*] proceeds from deafness our not hearing prevented our writing,—Jane, particularly, who is here a strict protestant, fearing that our letters should turn catholics and cross each other on the road. However now we each have something that will answer,—and accordingly I write to you, this time, lest by addressing Mrs. D. again, I should make you a green-spectacled monster, though I have matters fitter to write to the she D.—than to the He one. At all events I will write *at* her, in my description of such things as Balls and New Year's Eve festivities.

You were right in your prophecy about me, derived from my former letter[;] excepting a little exhaustion, partly from anxiety in getting it off, after my last box of cuts, I have regularly progressed in health, from the epoch I marked[?] of my strange malady.—Never indeed did I complete the Comic with such ease and satisfaction.[3] Except that I am more in figure a Greyhound I came in like a Spaniel winning the Derby, fresh & full of running. Indeed I set to work directly on my Sketch Book with some matters not so well fitted for the annual as a sort of Bubble book I contemplate.[4] I could write a *monograph* on Co-

[3] The first *Comic Annual* (for 1830) had contributions from others, but in the nine years that followed Hood wrote all of the poems, stories, and sketches for it himself, and illustrated it with his own wood block comic sketches, no small task for a man who was ill much of the time. He seems to have invented the punning drawing which gave a distinctive character to the *Comic*.

[4] "*Bubbles from the Brunnens of Nassau* By an Old Man," published anonymously in 1833, was the work of Sir Francis Bond Head, later Lieutenant Governor of Upper Canada. It was a light commentary on German customs and manners in the spas. The "sort of Bubble book" which Hood eventually wrote was *Up the Rhine* (published 1840). In it he embodied much of his German experience as described in letters to Dilke and others. It is interesting to ob-

blenz. But the place is healthy—witness Jane whose legs have grown smaller, & Tom's whose ditto have grown larger—whilst my own promise to "calve" in the spring. At any rate I have abundance of *hock*. Then we keep better if not the best & most regular of hours,—we do not take our mittag—exactly at midday but at 2 or 3—& then I am away from evil company & bad example & too much wine,—in which particular I have brought in and carried a *reform-bill* which I paid at Christmas. And then, biggest of all the thens, I am away from that dreadful *personal* pressure which made the light work heavy & the short work long.[5] I have not the knocks and rings at the heart, as well as the gate, which startled the Present—nor the long forecoming shadows of the future Days, coming each after each, like the old English warriors *bill* in hand. There were the menaces of the harsh and the requests of the gentle each equally urgent, nay where all were [just?], the demand backed with kindness & consideration gave me most pain & inquietude. There was the agony of the potent will and the impotent power. I believe I may say I was never a *selfish* debtor for I paid away money when I had it & left myself

serve, however, that though he apparently admired the "Bubbles" book, which has much of the spirit and the style of Sterne, he did not after all follow it very closely. In fact, while in general Hood preferred Sterne to Smollett, he took the latter for his model in *Up the Rhine*, its epistolary form, its jocosity and horseplay, and even its characters strongly suggesting the influence of *Humphrey Clinker*.

[5] Hood here refers to the debts which oppressed his last months in England. Little is known of the cause of these except that, as he intimates here, he had lived somewhat above his means at Lake House, Wanstead, a more pretentious establishment than he should have undertaken to maintain on the uncertain income of a writer, and that he suffered financial losses at the end of 1834. (See Introduction, p. 12.)

penniless almost, exposed to mortifications & deep annoyance for trifles. My struggles have been great & my sufferings unknown. I do not indeed forget my responsibilities here because they are not so often called for, & that I am out of the reach of legal measures, but I do feel released from the overpowering cares of a heavy expenditure & the transition from a hopeless to a hopeful state.[6] In spite of some sharp pangs in the process I am ready to confess that the crisis which sent me here was a wholesome one; although to do myself justice, I must say that without the absolute necessity I should have adopted some other course than that I was upon. I have been blamed I think not deservedly about Lake House,[7] by Judges from the event, but the truth is my prospects and standing were latterly completely changed—and I should have acted accordingly.[8] You may doubt but I can prove this fact in favour of my prudence. Some parts of your letter have set me feeling or thinking or rather have stirred up my feelings & thoughts, for they have been mine before—and led me to speak thus. If not as a thoroughly independent man (I mean morally, for I am so here actually) I have felt at second hand the

[6] The following lines were written on the side of the page beginning at this point: "dirty bread balls—toothpick stuck up in them &c.—I took a great disgust at him originally. I have just learned he is a Russian spy." They are obviously out of context and their reference is obscure. There is, however, mention in another letter to Dilke (May 19, 1835) of a man in a restaurant in Coblenz who stuck toothpicks in dirty bread balls. (*Memorials*, I, 91-92.)

[7] See p. 30.

[8] Hood here refers to losses suffered in 1834 from the failure of a firm in which he apparently had invested money. (See Introduction, p. 12.) It is probable that the sum for which Hood was liable was not great, and that he chose, like Scott, to assume the whole responsibility rather than take the easy way of bankruptcy. Eventually he did pay all his debts, either before or just after his return to England.

inestimable blessing of being *free;* which can hardly be said of anyone in England in the circumstances you allude to, to which I am in *some* degree a martyr. The struggle to maintain caste is indeed a bitter one & after all I fear we must say "le jeu ne vaut pas la chandelle." The aspiration for "the peace the world cannot give" is a really heavenly one;—though I doubt whether the world cannot give a very heavenly peace, if a man seek it the right way. At least I felt it could on my recovery for the first time in the balmy air of August taking a cheap ride to a cheap dinner along the banks of the beautiful Rhine to Capellen—& again further on in the harvest season thro the cornfield—vineyard—orchards to Braubach with *all* my happy healthy family in the same vehicle. It is true I miss *home*—old friends—books *the communion of minds*—& I cannot, I would not forget I am an Englishman. I love my country dearly and a sonnet I shall send you is one from the heart's core not the head. Oh Dilke tis the pity of all the pity's of the world that "that sweet little Isle of our own" should be what it is! Jane says in one of her letters what a pity there is not a cheap Coblenz in England—but why should not all England be a Coblenz? There never was a more senseless cry raised than that for taxing absentees, nor more unjust! But for our intolerable taxation there would not be those absentees—indeed some of our imports make me blush. For instance the other day Rampone [9] the Italian took up a

[9] Spelled "Ramponi" in the published letters in the *Memorials.* Though they had not much in common, he was one of the few "speaking" acquaintances of the Hoods during their first months in Coblenz. Hood had not much of an ear for languages and learned only a few words and phrases of German during his residence of two years in Coblenz. Rampone knew little English and Hood spoke no Italian, but they were able to converse in French which they both knew passably.

pocket-book & in the first page there was price 2ˢ/3ᵈ—duty 1ˢ/3ᵈ.—I can hardly think but that many reformers *must* have been made amongst the thousands that come up the Rhine, by the direct contrast of cheap and dear. Indeed I said in a letter to Wright [10] that it was enough to cause a pocket-revolution, not that the people would wish to remove their *monarch* but that their *sovereign* should go further.[11] Perhaps the police did not understand my *calembourg*,[12] for of all my letters this alone miscarried. Still, I *do* hope in the bottom of my heart to return honourably to England,—where I do believe a man may live comfortably, with some diminished feeling as to caste, if he preserve character. No matter how plainly he may live, should *he pay his way* he ought to be & I conceive would be, respectable. Still I shall be in no hurry to leave here—peace permitting—in duty to my children I ought to save all I can —but it is questionable when free to do so, whether for business sake I should not be amongst you. But of that hereafter. I am writing seriously because I trust my serious will give you as much comfort as my comic, for I conceive myself now to be in the right path. I would give anything for a day's talk or two—writing is so unsatisfactory but from what you have you must & perhaps can grasp the rest. I think there is no reason to be dissatisfied with the experiment. Coblenz is dearer than it was,—& will be cheaper. The English rush is falling off. But as it is we have done well.—In spite of illness inexperience and outfit—we have lived at but a trifle over 200 a year—I shall know better

[10] John Wright. (See p. 27.)
[11] This pun was repeated in a letter to Mrs. Dilke. (*Memorials*, I, 93.)
[12] Hood meant to use the French word for pun—*calembour*.

when the Doctor & Apothecary's bills come in.[13] All the three extra items I have given have been heavier than you might suppose. Rent is very dear here contrary to what you supposed. The population is not great but the large military garrison brings a quantity of officers into lodgings —indeed fresh houses are building—& furnished lodgings are especially rare. When I came there were hardly *any* to be had. The best plan is to buy furniture and sell it by auction when you go away, often for as much as it cost—but then I had not spare money so to lay by. Then till we got a kitchen the sending for portions to a Hotel cost us double to what we could cook at home—as to outfit we have had to buy glass, crockery, tinware &c., which does not come into their furnishing, & I had not a shirt in my bag that was wearable,—and we have bought children's clothes &c.— My illness will cost something considerable tho cheap by comparison—and in order to *discount* my recovery, for I was dreadfully low and languid, I felt justified in taking more wine than I should have done if well—and it answered the purpose. Lastly experience has had to be paid for—as for instance our washing is now done at half the cost for the first three or four months & almost everything is down from 25 to 50 per cent. Indeed the *dead set* at the English is to an extent nobody but a resident can discover—& really disgusting considering the great benefactors they are to the place; and that it is accompanied with envy jealousy and detraction, utterly illiberal.[14] I speak advisedly & from full

[13] Hood was frequently ill during his residence in Coblenz. (See Introduction, pp. 10-11.)

[14] Hood had a great deal to say of the fleecing of the English by the Coblenzers. (See the letters to the Dilkes from Coblenz in Chapters II and III of the first volume of the *Memorials*.)

knowledge. The Vertues [15] who resided here before us were *done* through thick and thin & yet he was a merchant, a smart active little man of the world with all his eyes about him & somewhat mean & with a family of 12 that made him cut close. But *we* know they were cheated. In fact the Coblenzers are Jews (if that be a term of *reproach*) stopping only short of giving you bad money or legerdemain in the giving the articles. Tis not cheating but next door to it. One day in joke I offered a fruit-girl ¼ of what she asked. Jane said I had affronted her & she would never come again—but she did—& we have had a bargain in something like that proportion. I could forgive this—but spite of all their sentimentality there is no *feeling*. I told you I gave a dollar to two begging catholic priests as a token of my wish for universal toleration & liberality of opinion. Ever since every German beggar is sent up to me,—some literally better dressed than myself—but I have laid down as a rule not to give a pfenning the 12th of a penny to any but a countryman. And why? Of all the cases I have had here, not one Englishman has ever owned to asking or at least getting anything of the Germans. The consequence is Mrs. Ainsworth [16] & myself, are the he and she English *consuls* of the town— Her husband is almost always travelling & she is the only other English resident. We send our distressed country people to each other & they get relief on both sides which is all they get. My blood boils & I hope I shall never

[15] An English family who helped Hood get established in the house at 372 Castor Hof in Coblenz before Mrs. Hood arrived with the children in the summer of 1835. (See *Memorials*, I, 58-59.)

[16] Unidentified. Might she be the wife, or a relative, of William Harrison Ainsworth, who, before he had made a reputation as a novelist, published Hood's *National Tales* in 1827? Ainsworth had separated from his wife in 1835, but there is no evidence that she was living in Coblenz in 1836.

hear again of subscriptions in England for distressed Germans. I will only mention one indisputable case. About three weeks ago Mrs. Ainsworth sent me a poor Irishman his wife and child—on their way to England— He had been engaged in a small manufactory of his own at Jonsac[?] in France which caught fire & he lost a child in the fire as well as having his arm burnt to the bone as he showed me in the attempt at rescue—and was deaf from falling on a beam. It was attested by Lord and Lady Ganville whose hand I know, Louis Philippe & a French Bishop & sundry English names.—The poor fellow, Irish all over,—in search of a rich English benefactor who lived at Frankfort had set out for Frankfort on the Maine instead of Frankfort on the Oder,— his wife lay in by the road,—and incurring some trifling debt in consequence even their *shoes* were sold & he was sent in irons to Frankfort. By the German law, necessaries cannot be sold for debt—chairs, table bed or working tools (England might take a hint here)—and Cartwright, our Minister at Frankfort was so indignant that he tore up Pat's passport (I suppose *branded with poverty*) & gave him another. In the list of donations he brought there was scarcely a German name—he said he had found it useless to ask them—and what had they done for him at Frankfort? Lest Cartwright should stir in it, the police took the mat out of his bed & never left him till the boat sailed with him hitherward.—Here he was advised by a German (who only gave advice) to apply to a rich wine merchant who spends six months a year in England & has made a fortune out of that little island. He gave him nothing. We gave him a trifle, & I gave him all the use of my name—& Jane had coffee made for the poor woman and her infant—they had to travel to Rotterdam on foot through bitter weather—& what was the result? The sneers of our servant—who could not disguise her spleen, & the refusal at the Hotel to admit him to see an Englishman to whom I sent him. This is too true & I assure you but a sample of the rest. Never may the English be such asses as to be liberal where they are only laughed at for it. I could allow for national prejudice, envy & jealousy, but they are so amongst themselves. There was a woman drowned her child here because she could not maintain it & herself though she worked hard, on some very low earnings. There was no established or private charity in the town to save the life of an infant!—& here everybody almost knows the other & their means. Damn their sentimental tenderness—where is the practical? On the back of this English affair, as we had assisted a countryman (Pat is & shall be my countryman if only for Taylor's sake) [17] came a modest request from a friend of our landlady's that we would *lend* her 10 dollars—*because* none of her own neighbors or country people would lend her 10 groschen. She was honest enough in her confession,—& if I had had them to spare I would have read them a lecture by lending them.—Then we had a poor Polish woman a lodger over head who was starving literally, for some money she had expected had not arrived *as might have happened to ourselves*. So we sent her some dinner daily in return for which she voluntarily knitted some stockings for Fanny, but her penniless state was the laughing stock with the servants. They *are* a heartless race set on the bawbees from high to low. Indeed in a thousand things language and all, I could fancy myself again, as when a boy, in Dundee. They have *some* of the virtues, all the vices & most of the peculiarities of the Scotch. Above all they are dreadfully beastly filthy horribly dirty & *nasty*. I have some stories on this head to

[17] W. Cooke Taylor, an Irish journalist who was a staff reviewer for the *Athenaeum* while Dilke was editor.

tell you *orally* that will disgust but make you laugh. Then they are stupid & like all stupid people intensely obstinate. Franck [18] says there is not a carpenter in the town can make a common guncase. They do not often show themselves drunk, but between wine & smoke their heads are in a continual *muddle*. There is a great sort of dog here which you see driving a calf not so big as himself—kept exclusively for that purpose that the butcher may walk behind with his pipe in his mouth.[19]—But I will give you a laughable instance of their dullness. The general opposite had ordered some great poplars in his yard to be cut down & we saw the whole operation. Each tree was nearly *cut thro* with the hatchet some ten yards from the ground by a fellow on a ladder which rested against the stem a dozen feet *above* the cut. I expected an accident every moment. The head gardener, pipe in mouth, looked on and superintended. The first tree all but lashed them in its fall—there were 12 men & 4 trees & twas a two days' job. At last came one of the biggest poplars in its turn. I saw even from my window & predicted that the rope would break, there was a join in it, —a knot, with a streamer of loose tow hanging from it— that could not be mistaken. Down they all went accordingly on the rugged stones—pipes & all—from which they got up looking very foolish and rubbing their behinds.

[18] Lieutenant Philip De Franck, of the 19th Polish Regiment of the German army, was stationed at Ehrenbreitstein near Coblenz. His mother was English and he had been educated in England. The chance meeting with De Franck (described by Mrs. Hood in a letter to Mrs. Elliot—*Memorials*, I, 76-77) was a most fortunate circumstance for the Hoods. During their residence in Coblenz he was their only intimate friend among the Germans and was a great comfort and help on many occasions. Speaking with equal fluency both English and German, he often acted as interpreter for his English friends.

[19] Described in *Up the Rhine*, pp. 189-190.

However they only tied another knot & tried again; the head man, & one or two who had looked on lending a hand. Down again,—as a matter of course. Jane & I shrieked with laughter & they evidently heard us. Well, what does a foggy headed fellow do, but go into the house & bring out a coil of literal *cable* fit to pull down a church with, & what do they do with it, but tie it at the end of the old rotten rope, & then haul away again! Twas a miracle they had not a third summerset,—but the tree thought proper to give away—there was a dozen heads together, in spite of the proverb no better than one! This ignorance as usual is joined to its Siamese brother conceit. I ventured to praise their method of applying leeches here which is good,—when the operator turns round on me & says "Now then Sir you can write to England & tell them how to put on a leech." I could have retorted that they could not make a blister as poor Jane found to her cost—for nothing of it *drew* except a wall of cobler's wax round the edge—as round a copper plate when being bit in. You see I am writing with my bristles up—but not without cause. There is a daily *nay hourly* skirmishing with our great chinese looking servant—from these national attributes—equally vexatious & ridiculous. But I find I must write to Mrs. Dilke, I have so much in her line,—so she shall have particulars. We have twice well scolded Gredle [20] thro Rampone & Franck,[21]—but last night Jane's patience gave way & she got into a towering spluttering Anglo-German passion, of ludicrous eloquence, that astounded the two maids—for we have a

[20] The Hoods' German maid in Coblenz, whose name (sometimes spelled Gradle) occurs frequently in the letters from that city. Writing to Dilke on May 6, 1835 (*Memorials*, I, 84), Hood says: "her name is Gradle, the short for Margaret."

[21] See p. 38.

second for a few days to assist in weaning. It was all about the English & German modes of that same—but Jane made use of an argument I had hinted & it was a floorer, namely "Vat can kennen, twey young maidkins, unmarried, so as you, mair den me, a Mutter of a Family of vaning de bibi—Have du Bibi? Have Lina Bibi" As Gredle has to my knowledge a bibi—mind it is two years old before I came—& Lina most probably has—it was a settler. On the next occasion I am to try my powers of scolding, indeed I have my own grievances and as Gradle's knowledge of English always deserts her when we scold, & she takes refuge in obtuse German, I mean to act a passion & be the English "God Dam" personified. I am quite in the humour for a flare up. My Apotheke bill has come in whilst writing, with its 18 groschen for emulsion—& *4 shillings for an elixir!* Then the doctor in respectable practice here—what would you think in England of a medical man who took advantage of his patient being a foreigner to charge double fees? But it is fact. I *know* it. These things deserve exposure—& it shall come out if I live—I am no he Trollope,[22] but I am indignant at the bad feeling against the English. Franck, an excellent witness for he was bred from boyhood in Germany, & his father is a German (his mother English) cor-

[22] Mrs. Frances Trollope, mother of Anthony Trollope, was chiefly noted for her quite illiberal and disparaging *Domestic Manners of the Americans* (1832). It is curious that though Hood here used Mrs. Trollope's name as a symbol for the English traveller of the complaining Smelfungus variety, he later found her judgment of the Germans much too favorable. Apropos of the boorishness of the Coblenzers, he wrote to Dilke on June 20, 1836: "I wish I could with honesty write more in the tone of Mrs. Trollope, whose book [*Belgium and Western Germany*, 1834], by the way, I have just read; but although, so treacley, it does not please the natives. Heaven knows why, for she does not object to one thing in Prussia, but the smoking." (*Memorials*, I, 159.)

roborates me. He says they are inconceivably jealous & envious of us & malicious accordingly. The other day he commissioned me to get for him the Book of Beauty [23]— which I found out was to be used in repelling the taunts of his brother officers, who if they see an awkward queer ugly woman of any nation but their own say—"there,—she is English." So I sent for a portrait of Lady Blessington to help us. As you are a gallant and gay man, pray get Caunter to send me some beauties out of the Court Magazine to fight on our side.[24] Then comes that d—d Rampone [25] the Italian with whom I have fought over again the battle of Waterloo, where we were all to be écrasés—only but that Bonaparte "had not time for it"—having vainly tried all day. But the forms this jealousy takes are so ludicrous it provokes as much laughter as spleen & I enjoy the conflict. He asked me seriously one day, when I set up our Navy against the Continental Army, whether an English captain ought to run away from a French ship. I answered he would certainly be tried, if of equal force, & perhaps shot. Well, then he gave me an instance in point. A French frigate was building at Genoa—and an English captain sent in a polite message by a fishing boat, that when she was in fighting order, they need not stop to paint or decorate her, which the English understood best—but to send her out. Accordingly, when the two English frigates had sailed off, or *taken flight* in opposite directions, out came the frigate

[23] An annual edited by Lady Blessington, "embellished" with engravings of paintings of famous English beauties.

[24] The Reverend John Hobart Caunter, a literary journalist who wrote pious verse for the annuals and reviewed frequently for the *Athenaeum* in the 1830's, must have had some connection with the *Court Magazine*, which occasionally "embellished" its pages with pictures of the fashionable ladies of the day.

[25] See p. 32.

with 2 more to take care of her, when to the confessed horror of the whole place, the two fugitives retraced their
course & a third appeared in the offing,—enclosing the three
in a triangle, so as to *force* them to fight which ended as
usual in their capture and destruction. I have taken this
engagement for my model—& lead him forth into deep
water and then give him a broadside of good hard facts. I
venture no theories or assertions. Luckily the other day
among some other papers came a *double* Times—with
which I astounded him,—as well as some of our statistical
tables—&c—& as he had held a meanish opinion of London,
its size and population, I sent him home with 14,000 rabbits
sold weekly by one salesman of Leadenhall, sticking in his
Italian gizzard. Apropos of this Italian. With all our faults
he is anxious to get some money out of us by teaching
French, Spanish, & Italian at London—with the slight draw-
back, that, like Goldsmith's attempt—he does not know the
language of his proposed scholars.[26] I told him moreover
that we had such swarms of refugees of education & rank
even I feared language masters must be drugs with us—but
I undertook to get a better opinion than my own—*So pray
in your next write me a sentence I can read to him.* Touching said Double Times—Dr. Beerman who called with a
New Year compliment saw it & I could get nothing said
for it—but an insinuation that the English could not be in-
dustrious if they read such papers—with an excuse that the
Germans had not such papers *only* because they had not
time to read them. When he saw my woodcuts, he took
great pains to impress on me that woodcutting was a Ger-

[26] Primrose in *The Vicar of Wakefield* (Chap. 20) arrived in
Amsterdam in the utmost confidence that he could make an easy
living by teaching English to the natives of that city, having forgotten that he knew no Dutch.

man invention from Albert Dürer, though I made him confess I could neither get wood here for love or money, nor if they had wood could they saw it and give it the surface. I am not writing thro spleen or prejudice but one has a right to retort on impudence and insolence. Nor do I mean to include others in one sweeping condemnation. I speak only of this place—what I have seen and heard. I know the English are made the standing joke of the coffee-rooms. Nay I have heard the Zeitung publicly read aloud at the table d'hote of the principal hotel with shouts of laughter at the expense I was informed afterwards of the English. This I take for gross ill manners, to say the least of it. But there is a vile spirit here against us—I believe elsewhere also. In the German dictionary Rickets is called expressly *The English complaint*—but what is the fact? [27] Travellers too often look only at the same things—churches, scenery, &c. one after another—nursing diet, & other matters of infinite importance being beneath their notice. Besides they press too hastily to see into such things. It would really make your heart ache here to observe the immense proportion of deformity—not in the lower class merely but the middle one—the children of tradesmen for instance.—The number of literal dwarfs—the wretched crooked, humped objects— the crippled children—the stunty bandy, bowlegged huge headed manikins & womanikins that swarm the streets—not of Fanny's stature, with 12 year old faces.[28] For a bet I would produce 20 from the neighborhood of those years without her height. But their legs & feet—I am not exaggerating—tis a sight full of pity & pain, to see so many foredoomed almost to helplessness through some great radical

[27] Hood made capital of this in *Up the Rhine* (p. 174).
[28] Hood's daughter Fanny was then five or six. She was born in 1830, but her birthday is not known.

defects in management on the part of parents. I never saw so melancholy a sight in my life, as they present—but the amount of this misfortune is immense and incredible—they are blind to it from its being like the dirty scabbed scalps of the infants, all but universal. It is literally shocking and disgraceful—and the result is seen in the numerous deformities and cripples—and a stunted ill made population. For one man above our average standard there are ten below it— "squat, my lord, squat—and bad on his pins." N. B. This without reference to Jane's quarrels about Bibi—although with such results before our eyes we might well have a horror of the system. Let them look at home. I have taken some sketches—veritable portraits in illustration which would astound you. Some day you shall have them, by a private hand, but remember these are all subjects in reserve for a volume, à la Head [29]—so do not let anybody forestal my observations. Mind, not a volume of prejudices—there are many things here we might & ought to copy—& after all my view embraces only a certain circle with Coblenz for its centre. Whilst on the German theme,—I must tell you how delighted we were with Bettine on the first notice of her letters in the Ath[m] & how disappointed and disgusted with her in the second.[30] Of her talents there can be no

[29] See pp. 29-30.

[30] Elizabeth (Brentano) von Arnim (1785-1859), nicknamed Bettine or Bettina, had formed a romantic attachment for Goethe when she was only 15 and continued to write to him for a number of years. He was temporarily charmed with her when they met in 1807 but later grew bored with her attentions and jealousies. Hood here refers to her *Briefwechsel Goethes mit einem Kinde* (1835), a highly colored account of the affair, which had been reviewed with fulsome praise and copious extracts in the *Athenaeum* (Oct. 10, 17, 31, 1835; pp. 754-757, 772-774, 814-816). The feverish Wertherism of her letters quoted in the second notice—and still more in the third— might well have disappointed and disgusted Hood.

doubt—but like Patmore [31] who apparently sacrificed Scott to the éclat of a duel, so did Bettine sacrifice, or suffer the martyrdom, of Gunderode [32] her friend, to the éclat of the suicide—the romance. Like Charlotte kissing the pistols and dusting them for Werter! [sic] De Franck knows all about her. She is quite notorious at Berlin. After the manner of L. E. L. she affects to be the girl [33]—so young and innocent, that she lays her head on gentlemen's bosoms or sits on their laps, as my Fanny might!! [34] But she met with a re-

[31] Peter George Patmore, a contributor to the *London Magazine*, was the second of John Scott, its editor, when the latter was killed in a famous duel in 1821. Patmore had apparently urged Scott to the personal encounter with Jonathan Henry Christie, a friend of Lockhart, editor of *Blackwood's Magazine*, who had first challenged Scott after a caustic word battle in their respective magazines.

[32] Karoline von Günderode, poet friend of Bettina Brentano, killed herself in 1806 after the two romantic girls had steeped themselves in Goethe's *Werther* and deliberately cultivated morbid sensibilities. The whole affair is described melodramatically in a letter of Bettina to Goethe's mother quoted in the third *Athenaeum* notice of the *Briefwechsel*.

[33] Letitia Elizabeth Landon, the most popular sentimental poetess of the 1820's and 1830's, whose initials were well known to readers of the *Literary Gazette* and the annuals, played the "innocent child," as Hood suggests, to the point where her engagement with John Forster, the friend and biographer of Dickens, was broken off by the resultant scandalous gossip.

[34] Bettina began early her unashamed practice of sitting on men's laps. In a letter quoted in the first notice of her *Briefwechsel* in the *Athenaeum* (Oct. 10, 1835, p. 755) she wrote of her first meeting with Goethe (she was then 21):

"I said suddenly—'I cannot remain any longer on the sofa,' and started up.

'Well,' he said, 'make yourself quite at home.' Immediately I ran and flung my arms around his neck; he drew me on his knee, and clasped me to his heart. All was silent—quite silent—everything faded away. I had not slept for so long; years had passed away in yearning toward him; on his bosom I fell asleep—and when I awoke, a new existence began in me."

45

buff. In the public theatre, she actually laid her head on the shoulder of a strange Polish officer,—who whispered to her, "I hope you haven't lice." She must lead her husband the poet a rare life of it! [35] Verily I am out of humour & confess it honestly, with all things German nearly but their country & their wine. There is Schlegel—Shakespeare Schlegel—in your last Athe[m] but one, truckling and lecturing at Vienna *for place*—nothing else.[36] I wish to like em but I can't. Perhaps I have here a bad sample—I suspect so for one fact speaks volumes. At the military casino you will see the officers of the 29th sitting separate each with his quantum of wine—those of the 19th—which is Franck's regiment—make a common bowl, as "banded brothers"— The 29th belongs to the neighborhood, & yet it has but about 1 in 4 of *volunteers* compared with the other. At the balls the Coblenzers are as decidedly in the background—but vide Mrs. Dilke's letter on this head. However I am a very loyal subject of the King of Prussia whose health I have drunk sincerely—and I have a really high opinion of him from what I hear. There are many things too in the army we ought to copy—for instance corporal punishment rarely ordered by sentence, & then inflicted only by three taps with a stick—the degradation of it is considered sufficient.

[35] In 1811 Bettina had married the poet Ludwig Joachim (Achim) von Arnim (1781-1831), the chief representative of the young romantics and a friend of her brother Clemens Brentano, also a poet of the romantic school.

[36] Hood apparently confused the two Schlegel brothers. August Wilhelm von Schlegel, friend of Madame de Staël and leader of romantic criticism in Germany, had made an excellent poetic translation of Shakespeare into German in the early nineteenth century. The lectures to which Hood refers, however, were given in Vienna in 1829 by Friedrich von Schlegel, younger brother of August. The English translation of these lectures on "The Philosophy of History" was reviewed in the *Athenaeum* on December 12, 1835 (pp. 925-927).

This is a fine spirited distinction, & what is more it *tells*. I am somewhat of Puckler Muskau's opinion as to the making every man a soldier here[37]—it has civilized them, in manners, feeling everything—at the very least mechanical gentlemen instead of 'practical' boors. You will laugh at my opinion on such topics—but I could write much on the army—and in its praise. What I have seen & know is admirable, as regards the infantry and artillery—of the cavalry I will say nothing—as they have no horses but what Reynolds[38] or I or you could ride & tis saying a great deal. Head is quite right about their rational system of harnessing, with the head and eyes free.[39] I have seen perhaps more than he, from the season of the year. Tis beautiful to see them exercising their own sagacity this frosty weather & picking out for themselves their way across a huge patch of ice before our window for which by the way in London his excellency our Governor would be fined every day of his life as it flows from his kitchen &c. But tho they have no spirit or skittishness the horses are hardy & enduring tho

[37] Herman Ludwig Heinrich fürst von Pückler-Muskau (1785-1871) was a picturesque soldier, traveller, dandy, gallant, and fortune hunter who achieved literary fame in 1830 by the publication of his *Briefe eines Verstorbenen* (Letters of a Dead Man). Hood again mentioned Prince Pückler-Muskau in the same connection in a letter to Dilke of June 20, 1836: "Good or bad politically, the making all men soldiers served to lick these cubs into human shape; it makes them cut their hair, wash themselves, and behave decently, in fact as Puckler Muskau says, the men, who have served, and those who have not, are different animals indeed." (*Memorials*, I, 159.) In seeking ideas for his German book Hood had probably been reading the Prince's *Tour in Germany, Holland & England*, translated by Mrs. Sarah Austin in 1832 (Vols. III and IV of the *Briefe eines Verstorbenen*).

[38] John Hamilton Reynolds.

[39] See pp. 29-30. Head discussed the merits of the German system of harnessing on pages 50 to 55 of the "Bubbles" book that Hood mentions so often.

slow, & were I to return to England to travel, single horse, I would accustom him, as here, to eat a loaf of brown bread, which you might stow in a gig far better than a truss of hay. Now—methinks I hear you say—Hood is amiable—for the last 5 or 6 pages he has been vicious—and of course he is softened & warmed by a glass of brandy & water. True as to that. But I was always notoriously illnatured in my cups—so set down all that follows to the credit of candour. I am going to praise the gendarmerie. I had watched & inwardly applauded their behaviour,—before I was told by Franck that they were all veterans, preferred to it by their general good conduct. I firmly believe it. As to espionage I know nothing, for I am not obnoxious to it—but in every other respect they seem to me to be a most effective & inoffensive police. I would rather have such a body than our raw lobsters, &c.—men who for the novelty of shedding blood make such massacres as at Peterloo & [Sptl?] Fields.[40] Two instances of police & law process here might put ours to shame. Vertue during his one year's residence was robbed of his plate & had the ill luck to receive & pass a forged note for 50 dollars— In the first instance the thief was discovered & the property restored *without expense*—in the second he did not lose the value of the note & had no trouble about it, but saying whence he had it and where he paid it. In such matters we are *barbarians*. What

[40] The famous Peterloo massacre of 1819 resulted from the stupid brutality of the "yeomanry" and "hussars" (a sort of gendarmerie composed of untrained business men) who charged into a crowd of some 60,000 defenseless persons including women and children, gathered near Manchester to demand the reform of Parliament. Several hundred were killed or wounded. The reference to Spitalfields is not quite so apropos. The riots of the Spitalfields weavers in 1767 were conspicuous examples of brutality and love of violence and bloodshed but were not directly the result of the actions of the police.

a contrast too is their debtor law, leaving the artisan his bed, his seat, his table & his tools of trade, attaching only superfluities & luxuries, to our White Cross Street atrocities & our Rich men living luxuriously in the rules. By the bye the Jerdan story—his application to you for character &c. is astounding!— [41] The net is plain, a plan to entrap same easy rich man into marriage with his daughter—but the application to you reads to me like a drunken audacious Garrick Club or Beefsteak Joke!!! [42] Are you sure it is not one of your own on an innocent at Coblenz? After that, come any thing. Is the day fixed when Wentworth & Agnes Jerdan are to be united? [43] I will come to that wedding anyhow. I must believe you—but after that I think I can play the

[41] Astounding indeed, if the reference here is, as seems probable, to William Jerdan, editor of the *Literary Gazette*. In the early 1830's Dilke had waged an uncompromising war in the columns of the *Athenaeum* on literary puffery, many times taking the *Literary Gazette* to task for its shameless puffing practices. (For further details see the second chapter of my *The Athenaeum: A Mirror of Victorian Culture*, 1941.) That Jerdan was not above social climbing is made evident in a brazen letter which he wrote to Prime Minister George Canning in 1827, offering to influence writers in Canning's interest, if in return he might be helped to "a somewhat higher station in society." (*Ibid.*, p. 120.)

[42] The Garrick Club, started in 1831 "for the purpose of bringing together the 'patrons' of the drama and its professors, and also offering literary men a rendezvous," had a reputation for late hours and conviviality. The Sublime Society of Beefsteaks was founded in 1735. It was in Hood's day given over to much badinage, foolery, and horseplay. Authors were mercilessly chaffed when they dined at the Beefsteak.

[43] Wentworth was Dilke's son, Charles Wentworth Dilke II (born in 1810). Is he the "easy rich man" whom Jerdan wished to entrap into marriage with his daughter? It seems hardly likely. The greater probability is that he merely wanted to make use of Dilke's good name to further his interests with another, and that Hood's suggestion of a union between Wentworth and Agnes Jerdan was only his jesting way of indicating how ridiculously absurd he considered Jerdan's proposal, whatever it was.

Boa with a whole rabbit. Bismallah!—(I ought to say Potz-tausend!) To proceed. There is another paramount subject here we ought to get a wrinkle from on our blushing brows —I mean general education. It is I believe obligatory for all children however poor to know the rudiments & the means are provided. But this subject is in abler hands.[44] Yet I must tell you how De Franck & I compared notes, for he had been like myself (at great expense), sent to first rate Private Schools, where,—we learnt nothing. I hope you will some day meet that you may hear him on that head—and the figure he cut when he went into the Royal School at Berlin. He is really an acquisition to us and I like him much. Tho a young man and soldier & gay—& fond of his joke, & mine—well principled, gentlemanly, an ardent lover of his country, unassuming, temperate—one I feel sure you would like & do hope you may meet.[45] God grant you may come next year—I see an advertizement of the Batavier from London to Mayence only £4.1.0!! I feel sure the Moselle is as fine if not finer than the Rhine—& not to be selfish, or I should wish for you earlier, the royal review here will be worth seeing as a picture of war. It is still doubtful but

[44] Hood probably refers to the work of Dilke's friend Mrs. Sarah Austin, who in 1834 translated the report on the "State of Public Instruction in Prussia" addressed by Cousin to Count Montalivet. In the preface she appealed to the English to profit by the example of Prussia in national education. She made a careful study of German institutions during her residence abroad and sent considerable foreign correspondence to the *Athenaeum*. When Hood wrote this letter she was living at Bonn.

[45] Dilke did meet De Franck when he and his wife visited the Hoods in Coblenz in Sept., 1836. Apparently the Dilkes were in Coblenz from the middle of September until after the middle of October. Hood left on his tour with De Franck's regiment on Oct. 11, before the Dilkes departed for England. (*Memorials*, I, 192, 198, 208.)

should the King not come the Prince Royal may. I shall know in good time. Would it were tomorrow our mutual tasks accomplished!

That last phrase has set my thoughts in a serious mould— & so let us to business. All this is supposed to pass in that family circle *of your own* into which you have confidentially invited me, & wherein I find myself with such delight. So to business. I must first of all as to the past not only beg you to give me credit for the best intentions, but the best exertions under my extraordinary circumstances that you may enter into my plans for the future. In the first place as to the Comic I stand better than I did last year in means & comfort, & materials for an early publication—I will not say before 1st Sept.—which will be in time for American export & here let me say I have a notion of dedicating to Washington Irving whom I know personally adopting Willis's [46] principle that tis the duty of every writer to lessen the distance between the two countries. It will be with me matter of policy as well as sincere feeling. And here as a corroboration of my notion of Tilt's [47] villainy let me first mention the following. I sold 500 of my first annual (with Hurst & Chance) to America. Of the second I sold some more, having been applied to *myself*, for some. After that for three years I sold none Tilt telling me there was no demand or that the Americans reprinted it. For the

[46] Nathaniel Parker ("Namby Pamby") Willis, the American poet-journalist, was a friend of Dilke and a close associate of several *Athenaeum* staff writers. In general, however, Hood had little sympathy with Americans. (See his caricature of the American in *Up the Rhine* and certain statements in his letters to Dickens—*Memorials*, II, 140, 141, 181.)

[47] Charles Tilt published the *Comic Annual* for 1831 and succeeding ones through 1834. Various quarrels of the kind indicated here led Hood to change publishers some months before he went abroad.

6th annual, in Baily's hands,[48] I have a demand again for 500—& amongst the letters sent out to me is one from Philadelphia with an offer of money for *early sheets* to reprint in Knickerbocker's Magazine of New York. It says, "You are every where admired in the best parts of America & your puns and sayings are extremely quoted. I think that the advent of your annual is a matter of as much moment in this country as that of the President's message."— Coupling this with the late order for 500 & knowing the Americans cannot well reprint for want of woodcutters, I think 'tis at least a suspicious case. However as I hope for an order for next book, the magazine forestalling will not do. As to Baily you are right—but I am in his power—& I believe he [*sic*] in money matters to be safe—a most important point. He is latterly very civil in his letters—he seems to have found out I am worth something to him—& I guess has published nothing else to any purpose. I shall hint to him my *opinion* on what he has done. And now to one main point. I have directed him,—after I am provided with money for next year, that I may have my mind at ease to do its best,—to pay over to *you* any balance due—*I have none else I can so well trust;*—and I fear attachments being laid at Baily's—by which the worst behaved & least needing might get paid before the better deserving. Would you take this trouble?—merely to hold it subject to my order to pay so and so. I conceive this might be better than a trifling dividend to all, & some I have heard from are both *able* and *willing* to wait. Others are necessitous—& one (not Martyr) barely honest, deserves to be last. My harvest this year will

[48] A. H. Baily became Hood's publisher in 1834, putting out the *Comic* for 1835 and succeeding ones. Hood finally quarreled with him too about 1840. (For Hood's side of the story see his letter to the *Athenaeum*, Oct. 17, 1840, p. 829.)

be a short one to what I hoped—but I thank God 'tis not worse. I feel what I can get thro with a free mind. I believe my last book to be a good one—for I made the most of my time when well. I have often gone to bed in the morning with my hand quite cramped with drawing—but they are a better set of cuts than last years. And now for your opinion—for you must be my guide. I should like not to run myself too close, in money for this ensuing year,—because a little *travelling*, leaving Jane &c. here would not merely advantage the Comic,—but I think I could make it pay generally for the eventual benefit of all concerned. The little I have seen has been of great use to me—tho I have not used all of it yet. I meditate some pedestrian expeditions hereabouts—but I want to see cities—capitols—men and manners.[49] I fancy I can make something out of them serious as well as comic—am I right? Pray write without reserve—in the confidential tone of your letter & indeed of all your advice to me—I can, will, take nothing ill. For my own part, I own to a strong impression—& it makes me regret former money misspent. Some may grumble but I seriously believe such outlay would be for the benefit of *all*. Tis not "a truant disposition, good my lord"—that inclines me to this wandering. I hope too not vanity but methinks even in this well travelled continent there is much to glean. I wish I knew the language but I am bad at learning tongues—& with my dulness of hearing do not catch the pronunciation. And now to the Club.[50] Am I not entitled to remain in it as a resident abroad without paying till I

[49] Hood's expedition with De Franck's regiment in the autumn of 1836, when he went as far as Berlin, was made use of in the later chapters of *Up the Rhine*. Incidents of the journey are described in the *Memorials* (I, Chap. 3).

[50] The Clarence Club mentioned below, of which Hood and Dilke were members.

return—if not,—ought I to pay up this year? I was one of the original members—& it would be pleasant & useful to me when I return. Apropos. Neither at the Clarence nor elsewhere did I ever see a *red* wine from these parts tho some are excellent as the Ingelheimer. But there is one worth your attention & I think the Club's perhaps—but it is not very generally known here. Franck who goes to reviews in the Eifel & has been marched & quartered all round about told me of it—& I have tasted it. It comes from the banks of the river Aar, a small rapid trout stream that falls into the Rhine near Andernach. It is bright, beautiful in colour,—quite rosy—& excellent in flavour. I prefer it to any claret I ever tasted. So would any one, I think, like yourself, who is fond of rhenish wines. It also bears transport better than other reds (which are somewhat ticklish in that particular) & cheaper. The price here—best quality—per dozen, bottles included, is five dollars— It seems to me so excellent that I have purchased a case of two dozen which when our steamers go again some time next month you will receive. If you will not accept it at my hands, you may repay me in the shape of a Cheshire Cheese some day:—but I would rather you would take it, & give me credit only for good taste. I have of course no purpose to serve—but as you dispense much wine hospitably I think it would be worth your notice as good and cheap and *a novelty*. I believe it ranks among the *Palatinate* wines. N. B. I drank some extra Hocheim on Xmas day which *un*naturally enough sent my thoughts *from* the Rhine to Grosvenor Place (Lower) [51] where I first learned to like rhenish. As to my sketch. I am glad you liked it—but your criticism is hardly criticism, as such—but matter of fact. The two

[51] Dilke's address in London.

parts—the foreground & distance—were separate parts, intentionally—the first is not literal—the second is, a portrait. —I intended to give *costume, uniform, sentry-box, barge,* &c. in front—considered per se—without reference exactly to pictorial effect—& yet, let me say—I almost believe to better eyes than mine, those objects might appear with as much distinctness—the distance from our window to the other side of the Moselle is not very great—and in the *early summer,* the air is peculiarly pure & *clear.* The distant hills *then* appear with all their minutiae like an elaborate coloured map. Had I generalized more the colouring ought to have had a different tone, as autumnal,—but when it was taken, I was struck myself by the *actual appearance* of the country, from the purity of atmosphere—exactly, as you express it, as if you looked at it thro a telescope. In the autumn come the extremely heavy dews which ripen and give *such a bloom* to the grapes. How I have longed to be able to paint a group of them! They are quite a study for colour. Every mountain almost produces its separate tint of green, tawny, purple—& many shades on one identical sort of grape according as each has been scorched by the sun on its peculiar soil. You might erect them into a sort of thermometer. Paintings of fruit are generally very insipid,— but one day when a plate full of Muscatels & Rieslings &c. was set before me I could not help thinking the artist who could give them property[?] would be in a good school for colour. By the bye did you ever eat here a small peach —a skin very like a very dirty blanket enveloping it, but within of a rich crimson with a flavour rather bitter, but far to my taste preferable to some of our handsome potatoes called peaches? You see I find something to like here— where indeed as Byron says "All save the spirit of man is divine." [52] And I like some of the people too—that is to say the peasants. I admire their industry, frugality, & content and cheerfulness—they are better *to the eye* too. But I detest the townspeople. Jane I really believe is reconciled—& to tell the truth we live very comfortable & I am very philosophical & thankful. We have many cheap luxuries—& comparative ease of mind. I sometimes feel again what is a spring of the spirits. Then the cheap fine scenery. One of my great delights at Lake House was that lookout behind—in my mind's eye I saw it in its *purple bloom*, nay its "purple light of love," last summer—it was worth *some* money that home view—with Temperance, divided from the wine cellar by a pond.

I have said nothing yet of the Ath[m] or its notice.[53] The paper is a great treat to me—& latterly it has been more interesting than usual. You do not say but I hope indeed feel it must go on flourishingly. Wright says the reviews of the Comic are by J. H. R.[54] I own I cannot detect his hand. They read to me like your own. I predicted the Girls' Boarding School bit would be extracted,—and Miss Norman *has* my pet story—so I could not have been better pleased had I *reviewed myself*. The Ocean was written con amore—tho rather contra amore, too, for I *do* love the sea in spite of its last spite to me.[55] I miss its fish tho we get tolerable salt haddock & middling herrings & bad oysters. You cannot imagine how I adore shrimps even—now I cannot get 'em.

[52] *The Bride of Abydos*, Canto I, line 15.
[53] The *Comic Annual* for 1836 was reviewed in the *Athenaeum* of Dec. 12 and 19, 1835 (pp. 928-929, 942-944).
[54] John Hamilton Reynolds.
[55] Hood was nearly shipwrecked in a violent storm off the coast of Holland when he crossed on the *Lord Melville* in March, 1835. This crossing is described in letters in the *Memorials* (I, 52, 70, 82), and humorously in *Up the Rhine* (p. 17 ff.).

And Miss Seil [56] has ornamented our drawing room with a painting of a dutch fisherman at his stall, smoking his pipe—over a magazine of all sorts of scaly, finny & shelly eatables, —with a glimpse of the sea & a boat coming on with a fresh live cargo in the distance. Sometimes it makes me savage—& I curse his soul. Especially now—when there is no *hammel* flesh to be had in Coblenz—not ham but mutton.—Nothing but beef—fit to eat. The very huge pork & the very tiny veal is out of the question. Both are abominations. Especially to Farmer Hood who reared both calves & pigs of his own. The fun of it is, there is a great pig fair at Ehrenbreitstein in November,—after which all Coblenz eats pork & nothing but pork whilst the stock on hand lasts. I popped on a domestic party busy killing two hogs, for they are literally not porkers but bacon hogs, & Wanstead recollections came over me so as to make me laugh aloud, to the great disconcerting of the Master & Mistress. By the bye Franck tells me they have discovered a very active poison only second to *prussic* acid in *prussian* black puddings—several persons have died. Of course the pig blood was in a bad state. By the way, I suspect German pigs smoke actively as well as passively (in hams) they are so apathetic. I saw a whole barge load come over the Rhine & expected on the boat touching the shore after struggling thro the ice to see all the drove run away—but I was mistaken. They had no notion of running like Leigh Hunt's pig [part torn out with seal] ["up all manner of] streets"— [57] but each went quietly with its owner. [torn out] seemingly to their

[56] Daughter of Widow Seil, the Hoods' landlady at 272 Castor Hof in Coblenz. (See *Memorials*, I, 58-59, 78.)

[57] See Leigh Hunt's essay "On the Graces and Anxieties of Pig-driving."

education under some such [torn out] as Head describes.[58] We have had some sharp touches of [torn out] of the night tight froze. The middle of the lb. of butter—& a pie-crust Jane was making. It was once very intense—& as our back bedrooms look northwards over Rhine & Moselle, the stove there is not a good one & moreover that side of the house is slightly built, one night we actually decamped & all slept on a row with our beds on the ground in my little study. *Now* it is frost & thaw by turns, which is worse. The Moselle ice has given way and come down at a racing pace, but the Rhine is still frozen over at St. Goar. The *variation* is great & trying. I have a regular sore throat at 9 P.M. & Franck has one every morning. Every house almost has the measles in it & ours has not escaped. Poor Tom [59] has got them—and weaning & cutting his eye teeth at the same time. I am finishing this sitting up while Jane sleeps. I am almost ashamed of the length of it—for it will cost more than it is worth, but I shall not be able to write often.[60] I rejoice in your good account of the Doctor—I

[58] In the "Bubbles" book mentioned before (see pp. 29-30) Head describes German pig-driving in a chapter called "The Schwein-General." He, like Hood, observed the apathy and starved condition of the creatures: "their bodies were as flat as if they had been squeezed in a vice; and when they turned sideways, their long sharp noses and tucked-up bellies gave to their profile the appearance of starved greyhounds." (p. 97)

[59] Tom was about a year old when this letter was written.

[60] This was in the days when the recipient paid the postage charges on a letter. Before 1840, when Rowland Hill initiated the penny post, the rates were extremely high, never having been lowered since they were increased to raise revenue during the Napoleonic Wars. The postal charge on a letter traveling 15 miles was 4d., and there was a steep graduation of scales so that it cost the recipient 17d if he got a letter from a correspondent 700 miles distant. Moreover, one sheet of paper was considered one letter, regardless of weight or size, and two sheets counted as two letters. This may

wish we had only as good a mediciner here. Beerman tells
me they call Sydenham [61] the second Hippocrates,—but I
cannot edge in a word for the later professors. The Germans in Typhus give cold water—Franck says a little while
back cold water was the cure for all complaints—as they
clip all their dogs, foxdogs, wolfdogs, poodles, all sorts into
lions. Should *I* be ill again here I have made up my mind
to doctor myself & trust to nature & Providence.—I have
had a letter from Moxon [62] applying for letters of Lamb's
which he wants to publish. If you say aye to this he shall
have them.—But I meant them for your use. It is too late
now perhaps to write the article I proposed, but I think if
you could collect for me & save all that has been written
about him (C. L.) I could make a good review of it—cor-
roborating, contradicting & giving my own view. Pray
remember this in your next.[63] By the way, knowing all we
do of the affair—Moxon's sonnets to Emma read "Sufficiently fulsome . . ." [64] He sent them to Jane.

explain why Hood's long letters from Coblenz were written closely
on huge foolscap folios.

[61] Dr. Thomas Sydenham (1624-1689), English physician, whose
reputation rose more rapidly abroad than at home.

[62] Edward Moxon, "publisher of poets," was a close friend of
Lamb. Moxon apparently turned over the letters which he gathered
to Sergeant Talfourd for his *Letters, with Life, of Charles Lamb*
(published by Moxon, 1837). (See Harold G. Merriam, *Edward
Moxon, Publisher of Poets* (1939), pp. 66-69.) Whether Hood com-
plied with Moxon's request is not known, but he probably did not,
for none of Lamb's letters to Hood were published in Talfourd's
volume.

[63] Hood did not publish the Lamb letters in the *Athenaeum*, nor
did he write the proposed article about his old friend, but he did
later record at some length his recollections of Lamb in his "Literary
Reminiscences" in *Hood's Own* (1839).

[64] Moxon had married Lamb's adopted daughter, Emma Isola, in
July, 1833. What Hood knew of the affair it is difficult to guess,
unless he had heard the gossip that prompted Crabb Robinson's sug-

The measles have been so prevalent even several ladies have been prevented going to the Balls—by having them. Little Tom is well again after a three days bout of them. I have just received the Athe^m of 1st January. It is an excellent one—first rate. By the bye, I suppose I have learned to bow well here as you have borrowed my bow in the Comic for your Ath^m one at the end of the year.[65] I have not seen a Comic yet (the 17th) & we are anxious for the fate of a parcel to have been sent out before Xmas. Mrs. Dilke's letter will come by next post—after which I must write other[?] matters than letters. I wrote to J. H. R.[66] & he talked of writing to me but has not yet— All good wishes to you *all*—not forgetting *Lord Chichester* should he be in town—& with huzza for 1836 believe us Dear Dilke Yours ever very truly

Thomas Hood & Co.

Jane's love to Mrs. D. &

will write soon.

Since writing the foregoing a little newyear's gift of a needle case very pretty has come from Maintz for Fanny from our grateful little Pole. Fanny alone was on *speaking* terms with her. It has given us great pleasure, liking to have human nature redeemed as much as we can from reproach. De Franck has also brought me a present, a most useful one, an excellent case map of Germany & its adjacents—it is endorsed "to Mr. Hood from his friend P. de Franck, as a reward for trussing puddings"—"Thou shalt heap fiery

gestion (in which Moxon's biographer puts no faith) that Lamb "induced" Moxon to marry Emma. (For a discussion of the relations between Moxon and Emma see Merriam, *op. cit.*, pp. 50-53.)

[65] Dilke quoted from Hood's preface to the *Comic Annual* for 1836 a passage running the gamut of puns on the word "bow" as his final bow for the year in the *Athenaeum* (Dec. 26, 1835, p. 969).

[66] John Hamilton Reynolds.

coals on the head of those that betray thee." To understand
which mystery you must read mine to Mrs. D. Also the
operative-surgeon's. All has come in in English for me thus,
in one item "for his Lady. To put blood suckers at her
eyes—6 shillings" 6 times the regular charge—I am going to
dispute it. The Ice on the Rhine today (12th) is coming
down & de Franck is blockaded on the other side. We are
looking for some huge masses when it breaks up at St.
Goar. All Bingen has been and is under water. We expect a
flood 3 or 4 feet deep in Castor Street next to ours & the
engineers are contriving *rafts*. One day here was so suddenly warm nay hot, in the midst of the frost it was quite
annoying & made us all ill.

[Sturm und Gemütlichkeit]

"Prosit Neujahr!" 372 Castor Hof Coblenz.
12 January [1836]

My dear Mrs. Dilke,
When a lady writes to a gentleman that she "dotes on
his hand" and "adores his correspondence" he cannot do
less than let her hear from him again at the first convenient
or inconvenient opportunity. He ought to address her—
even instead of being introduced to the beautiful Miss
Doubt or Miss Hasebeck, or messing with the officers of
the 19th—dancing with Lena—scolding Gradle—gallivanting
abroad with de Franck—drinking Kissingen—ditto Rüdes-
heimer—waltzing—smoking—& other pleasures of the kind
—all of which I forego at the present writing for your sake.
I only hesitate—on account of the deep dip it must make
in your private funds for postage—but you must write an-

other Index or two for which you are so handsomely paid—
& make up the loss.[1]

Your "long and delightful" letters came to my hand at
the very fag end of the year which they helped to wear
out—and perhaps at no other moment during 1835 could
they have found me so out of myself. I was only dressing
to go to a grand New Year's Eve Ball (you know I don't
dance any more than the Tenth) [2] to meet all the rank,
fashion & beauty of Coblenz. Here methinks Dilke to
whom you have given this to read, lights a candle with it,
& suddenly goes off either to bed or to sit in his old recess
on the stairs. You know you could never get him to take a
ball—without a balling-iron—any more than a horse. Imagine my plight. Altho only half beautified, & regardless of a
bran [sic] new bright figured satin waistcoat, that cost me
four dollars—and as yet never tried on to see how it looked
—I jumped up and read your respected favours in my shirt
sleeves, but with my head well frizzed by Jane—meanwhile
de Franck in full feather with a cocked hat to it, awaited
my companionship. I really wished the new year put off
for another day—& indeed for a moment I feared my gaiety
was at an end. Happening to look up I saw Jane, red as a
turkey cock—her head thrown back against the wall, a letter on her knees, choking & chuckling as if going off into
hysterics at some fatal news. Luckily, it proved to be only
Mr. Lind's bell that wrung her so, and you may suppose I
went off to the Ball in good humour & spirits, thinking
every now and then of that unfortunate gentleman intend-
ing to go to Cork but finding himself in *Belfast*. My ticket
to meet all the rank and beauty & fashion cost only twenty

[1] Perhaps Mrs. Dilke made the index for the 1835 volume of the
Athenaeum.
[2] The Tenth Regiment probably (German or English?).

groschen, & it was worth every shilling of the money.[3] His Excellency General de Bostle,[4] Commander of all the Rhenish Provinces, was there,—and so was my tailor—& the man of whom I bought my black stock. To be sure altho in one room, there was a West End. The rank particularly occupied the top corner to the right, & the left corner next the door seemed to be the favorite with the snips and snobs. To do the latter justice, however, they behaved with much more decency & decorum than would have prevailed in such a motley assemblage in London. How would you stare too in London to see at a Ball, a score or two in the uniform of common soldiers, offering their partnership to the ladies— but the fact is as everybody must be a soldier in Prussia, & there is no purchasing commissions, some of these common soldiers are the sons of Barons. The dances were Waltzes— gallopades—& contredances—the last like our quadrilles. They mostly danced well especially the Waltz—which is such a favorite that I saw girls stand up for it—steady looking, decidedly serious as my sister Betsy whom I should as soon have expected to see whirl off with a young man, round a room, after some sixty other couples. They made my head spin at last with looking at them—but the music was beautiful & excellently played. I think I could at least have flounced about *in time* to it myself. The instruments were many and various. They seemed never to tire of the whirling:—and de Franck says they often waltz on those *polished* floors where we can hardly walk, without breaking a leg as the Duke of York did. I was amused to see de F. & a lady each

[3] The description of the ball here given was copied almost verbatim by Mrs. Hood in a letter to Mrs. Elliot (*Memorials*, I, 120 ff.). Hood also described the New Year Ball in *Up the Rhine*, though not in such intimate detail (pp. 131-132).

[4] In the *Memorials* this name is printed "Borstell."

63

pull out a card or little book & register something, much in the Tatler's old style of betting—it was an engagement to each other, to dance together at some certain ball, perhaps a month to come.—From time to time the company refreshed in a suite of rooms, laid out with tables—each company paying for its own. For my part I got pleasantly enough amongst a party of Franck's brother officers—one of whom instantly tendered to me a glass of *Cardinale*, i.e. Bishop (only cold) with wine, sugar, & the rind of a small green orange they grow here as large as a cotton ball,—and which has the peculiar property that a little too much of the rind in the mixture will infallibly give you the headache. Oddly enough,—when I looked in his face I recognized a tall strange officer, to whom I have frequently bowed by mistake in the street—which according to the etiquette here was returned by himself & all who happened to be along with him, so that I gradually got on bowing terms with half the officers in Coblenz. As he spoke French which I have picked up again, we had a little gossip—during which he informed me that Franck had let him taste some genuine English Plumbpudding [*sic*]—*but that it lay very heavy all night.* Whereby hangs a tale:—We were all hail fellow & hobbed & nobbed—& I told through D. F. the story of the *bell* which *told* very well. Instead of lobster salad I ate herring ditto & really it was very nice—much more than you would have expected from the fish. Jane's health was drunk:—but of course all on *my* account. The officers of the 19th are very popular—the ladies dance with them & the brothers enlist in their corps. For one blue or red epaulet there were nine or ten yellow ones [5]—& there is no little jealousy on these accounts amongst the other warriors. I wish I could say much for the beauty

[5] The yellow epaulets were apparently the distinguishing marks of Lieutenant De Franck's 19th Polish Regiment.

of Coblenz—but there were only, to my taste—three or four with any pretensions—one of those even with a complete english [*sic*] devonshire, face, & another black haired, on a minor scale a Mrs. Chatterly, if you remember her—decidedly anything but German. Her name translated is Miss Doubt. The great favorite is Miss Hasebeck,—the officers hardly reckon it a ball without her—yet she is not handsome —her nose is decidedly plain & nobby even—but she seems clever,—which is rare enough here I guess. I had also a little young wife of 16 pointed out to me as "very interesting"— but she looked too like a school girl. As to dress—you know how I always got scolded because after *your* parties I could never describe whether Miss A. or B. was in blonde or bombazine—so you must excuse the millinery—especially as being of all grades they wore all sorts of fashions. There was a Belgian officer present, who I hoped would dance, as they say he does it execrably—what a comfort for *me*—but he did not show himself up, that night. Perhaps as our old friend Mrs. Dilke used to say, "he had a hint[?]." At last came the dance I had come to see. Exactly at twelve—bang went a minor cannon in an adjoining room & the waltz instantly broke up, & the whole room was in motion—everybody walking or running about to exchange salutations, & kisses & embraces with all friends & acquaintance male or female— Such *hearty smacks*—such hugs—& handshakings—to the chorus of Proast Ni Yar! Proast Ni Yar! [6] Some of the maidens methought kissed each other most tantalizingly on the lips & neck, & languished into each others arms—I am afraid because so many nice young men and gay officers were by to see it—but then their fathers and mothers were as busy too kissing & bekist. With some of the older codgers it was

[6] Prosit Neue Jahr!

quite a ceremony & I should think the demand & consumption in the sentimentals was very great. And there, all the while stood your humble servant—the poor English creature—the disconsolate—the forsaken—Dummy—a looker on—what you will—with my lips made up and my arms empty—a lay figure—whilst the very fiddlers were hugging. Of course I could not embrace my tailor or kiss the man I bought the black stock of—but luckily I had recognized two young ladies I had *seen* at Vertue's [7]—(you see I stuck to the *virtuous* though Jane was *not* present)—we had never been on speaking terms—because they did not like to own to French *something like yours*. However I convinced them that mine was no better, & we complimented each other with a good deal of bad language. So I went and looked a salute at them, which made them smile—& then the tall officer came & shook hands with me,—& even this, which was my *all*, comforted me. De Franck told me his back ached with bowing. It was really a funny scene—& if you will give a New Year's Eve Party—& have plenty of beauty, rank & fashion, I will try to introduce the custom when I return. I mean to try to draw or sketch the scene—so you will see something like it. Dancing is much in vogue. Jane has a young girl to help whilst Tom Junior is weaned—not untimely, as the Bavarian beer, which was Jane's tap, has been stopped from coming by the ice.—Tis a fattish maiden, not with very "light fantastic toes" tho she always affects to walk on them,—& it turns out that on her early evenings when she leaves us precociously she goes to learn to dance of a Frenchman—whom she pays a dollar a month, her wages from us being two dollars per ditto. But *hops*, or balls as they call them, at the taverns prevail during winter, & the

[7] See p. 35.

young ladies of the lower class are not very steady or serious accordingly. By Franck's account, who has officially to visit such places, they must be like the dignity balls in the West Indies—hot, noisy, dusty, thirsty, & *very hard work*. In Poland sometimes the soldiers sing the tune to which they dance in chorus, doing double duty. As for Lena, our dancing maiden, her head runs so on her legs, she is all but good for *nothing* as to memory. Even Tom took such a contempt for her she was obliged to be turned into the kitchen in lieu of nursemaid—whereof came three lenten days running for us, seeing that, full of dancing, she could not keep the pot boiling or the meat broiling. Gradle in the meanwhile (like Leigh Hunt's pig) [8] set off down all sorts of ways of her own—as to child management—& you will read in mine to Dilke how Jane scolded her into the right road. I am afraid she too had been dancing & kissing & got tippy too on New Year's night—for instead of putting the boy to bed she was found lying on it with him in her arms & his cap off. However Tom is very fond of her—as far as regards her nursing—but as to her cooking he splutters her German broth out again without ceremony, & I do not wonder. It is toast & water, with a strong dash of onion, nothing more. He follows his father's good taste—and when *I* offer him anything he gapes like a young blackbird. I only regret that I was not present at Jane's Anglo German flare-up. It must have been a good one as for some hours after Lena walked sedately with her *heels* to the ground— & Gradle looked astounded. To tell the truth we are all of us made up for scolding, & what is called showing fight. We have found out so much cheating & jewish dealing we mean to speak our minds "bow wow skow wow anyhow"—

[8] See p. 57.

even Fanny who can't be kept out of the row nags some-times in German in which she is actually fluent— Nay hav-ing been tickled with the novelty of the *gutturals* she out-herods Herod, & never parts with a rough word till she has *well gargled her throat* with it. Seriously, as Lord Liverpool said, tis "too bad"—for thanks to Franck we are let into all the mysteries of their extortion. We were beginning to find them out ourselves & began to marvel how much longer one ten pounds lasted than its predecessors. But on com-paring notes,—our expenses with those of certain Colonels & Majors with which Franck supplies us—we are grossly *done*—as he says his own family was at first,—so we mean to take care of our bawbees as well as our baby.—When Jane returns to London you will never like to go shopping with her she will haggle so. For my own part I get savage and am for "beating them down" with a club. Then they are so pigheaded—we can hardly get what we like. Little Tom in spite of ourselves, if we had not been *very obstinate* too, would be flourishing about in a scarlet or skyblue em-broidered cap, with a gold tassel—and I am not quite sure when out of sight of the house, whether he does not wear his cloak inside out—a showy tartan lining being more pretty to their fancy than the maroon or claret cloth with-out. A pair of ink-spotted fawn summer trowsers I sent to be dyed black, but I have expected them to come home pea green or skyblue. Purple was strongly recommended. Pink wouldn't have been objected to. Rampone the Italian, who has married a German, says obstinacy runs in their blood— which hints much as to his domestic felicity. But it is very true. Gradle, who gives us our dinner when she likes, will argue with the clock staring in our faces that 3 is 2—so we are obliged to turn pigs like the swinish multitude & only after a good deal of grunting get our own way. To my comfort, all our tragics have a goodly proportion of farce along with them. Even the doctoring makes one laugh as well as cry.

You heard of Jane's inflamed eye—& her having a hot baker's sack over her head as a sudorific specific. Also her blistering and leeching. As you I believe also have "blood suckers at you" sometimes I will give you a hint how to avoid the trouble & tediousness generally of getting them to bite. Put them into a basin of tepid water, & let them swim about for 5 minutes which makes them lively & eager & saves much time and trouble—for they are beasts apt to bite when not wanted to do so, & vice versa. The unprinted leech story—which Wright [9] has toward next Comic refers to what really happened to Franck in Prince Radzival's Park. And now I will answer your question as to our Xmas dinner. We did not attempt a sirloin—which is not to be had, nor could we cook one with our apparatus. So Jane thought of a fillet of veal & never could you dream of such a noble festive display for the season. It came in, about as big as a plate! a dessert plate! I saw it ordered, & all the while Jane pointed out how it was to be cut, I saw the butcher shaking his chuckle-head behind her back & I predicted that he meant to have *his own way*. So he split it in half, & Dilke will have a notion what ½ the fillet of a Coblenz calf would be.—indeed Jane thinks I have exaggerated the size—however, I feel sure, Dilke with only one of his ordinary appetites could have eaten it all up:—and then asked for a plate of the boiled salt beef we fortunately had in addition. Perhaps also he would have put his lips moreover to our pig's-face. Those were the three courses. Thanks to Jane we had a plum pudding & a very good one

[9] John Wright. (See p. 27.)

—which Franck "took to heart" so that Jane afterwards made one for him.[10] You will not suspect me of jealousy—but I did threaten to pop some tenpenny nails or bullets into the composition, & Jane, who takes a joke as a pike takes a minnow, watched over her work with catlike vigilance. I could never get near the mixture,—and she stuck by it like a hen to her eggs till the pudding was fairly in the pot. Will you believe that after all, as she went to bed before me, she sent Gradle with it when done, to have it locked up in the drawing room where I was writing all alone. It was put down smoking under my very nose—& the spirit of mischief was irresistible. We had bought a groschen worth of new skewers that very morning. I cut them a little shorter than the pudding's diameter & poked them in across & across in all directions so neatly that Jane never perceived any outward visible sign of the inward invisible wood, although she stood and admired it for five minutes next morning before she sealed it up in white paper & sent it to Ehrenbreitstein. The next time Franck came he praised it very highly—I asked him if it was not well trussed —& he answered "Yes" so gravely that I thought he meditated some joke in retaliation & kept on my guard. At the ball the truth came out—he actually thought it was only some new method of making plumpuddings & gave Jane credit for the wood-work. You may guess I caught a rare scolding—not only at home, but when we went out it lasted all the way up Nail Street—to the text of "practical jokes are the lowest things in the world." And to this day Jane believes *almost* that the long officer who partook and complained of such uneasiness afterwards, had swallowed a skewer. Lord help their peaking german stomachs—they

[10] For Jane Hood's story of the pudding, see *Memorials*, I, 123-124.

think the English are perfect ostriches at digestion. Franck makes toast for his breakfast & tea, English fashion—& they complain that *that* "lies heavy." They ought to go to the Sandwich Islands where the cooks *chew* the victuals for the table. After dinner we had some good Hocheimer, for which at the Hotel they *would fain* have charged me 2½ dollars a bottle—at which price I could drink it I guess at the first Hotel in London— So we did pretty well for a Christmas dinner. But lent is coming—or rather *is* come. There is no mutton to be had.—and no ham. We tried a bavarian one the other day & it was literally like a pickled leg of pork. And the salt haddock are stopped—& the Bavarian beer. I miss the mutton which is better than the beef —coz why? The oxen go jobbing about the fields & roads before they are made beef of—& the cows even go out choring[?]. So the calves are killed at 9 or 10 days old poor things, mere flabby dabby babbies. As to beer the Coblenz-made is not good & I do not wonder. You see written up "Beer Brewery & Bath House" the mystery of which singular connexion I have only just dived into. For some complaints the Germans bathe in malt:—Good God! I should not wonder if they bathe in the beer. It certainly has an odd, very odd flavour. What a new way of giving *a body* to it. Fancy—only fancy a fat dirty brown stout gentleman, stuffed with garlic & grease & sourkraut—& well smoked with tobacco, sitting stewing in a vat of Krug & Co's entire! But you drink London porter. "Tant mieux for you," to quote a bit of your own French. I think here I shall have a triumph over the Brunnens man—[11] He has not mentioned *Swipes*—Bad amongst his Baths! Now for the Lurley-hurly-burly.

[11] See pp. 29-30.

The other day Franck told us all the Rhine ice after leaving Bingen had stuck fast at the Lurley [12] in a manner never seen within memory of man. Upon this hint we went, Jane, Fanny & I. Dilke knows the spot.—& I can show you some view of it—there is one in Tombleson's book.[13] It was a beautiful day for us & though the Germans who are apt to exaggerate had talked of icebergs not to be found the sight was well worth seeing. Imagine that narrow passage blocked up with a storm of ice—for the immense pressure had heaved it up in huge waves or furrows—eight or ten feet high: each ridge composed of massive slabs of ice tossed about in all directions—at every bend of the river there had been a dreadful scuffle & the fragments were thrust upward endways. But the mighty river would not be dammed up—you saw it now & then in a narrow slip rushing like a mill race,—then it plunged under the ice and boiled up again 100 yards further. We followed it to Oberwesel part of which was under water. This was but last week—but a steady thaw set in since & tomorrow the bridge will be replaced to the great convenience of the Ehrenbreitsteiners, who have had to pass in boats to and from the many balls at this gay season. Franck could never stay beyond ¼ to 9 at night. The Moselle ice carried away one foolish lad who was tampering with it—and a more romantic incident occurred on the Rhine. On an island just above this resides a Countess Pfaffenheim,—unfortunately neither young nor pretty enough to complete the romance—heaven knows what foolish process brought her to it—perhaps she was pushing the bits of loose ice along at the edge as chil-

[12] The more familiar spelling is "Lorelei."
[13] *Views of the Rhine*, edited by W. G. Fearnside, was published in London in 1832 by W. Tombleson and Company. An engraving of the "Lurleyberg" is shown opposite page 163.

dren do—but she managed to plump in. However some German cherub that sits up aloft, brought a willow bough to her assistance & there she hung well preserved in ice—a good long spell—till the genius of German romance brought to her rescue the son of a man who has been long at law with her father. I know not the denouement:—whether the suitor prevailed:—but how well she can enter now into the fancy of that Arabian Tale wherein the people, princesses and all had their lower half of cold marble. Jane was delighted with our jaunt—the scenery is so beautiful—& we dined at St. Goar very well & reasonably. In the river by St. Goar I saw some salmon. The Moselle & Rhine swarm with fish, & as the Germans don't angle, rods & lines go free. Franck & I mean to try our skill. Perch so large as to be sold by the pound—& in the absence of all sea fish they are valuable to us. Jack & Barbel abundant, & a large white fish peculiar to the water. So that fishing—a desirable item that Reynolds recommended—is here in perfection. Besides, independent of the sport, the perch are as dear as meat. I have just had some for dinner—& the Bavarian beer is come again—which I am glad of for Jane's sake. She works hard poor soul at times—should you know of any one who wants an excellent sick-nurse or nurse from the month—a good occasional cook & willing to make herself generally useful besides—can curl gents hair—take a hand at cribbage if required—act as amanuensis *over hours*—or reader—cut pencils—and other jobs in the fancy line—no objection to go abroad—& salary no object—so as she's in a small genteel not decidedly serious family—where no footman is kept—will undertake teaching the rudiments of reading & writing in lieu of nursery governess—also music—where there is a piano—can have an undeniable character for honesty, sobriety & industry from her first & last place—should you know of any one in want of such an invaluable creature—they shall have her when I *don't* want her. The invaluable creature by the way has just set me right about Countess Pfaffenheim. She is young—but not handsome. A chubby brick colour face thatched with tow-coloured hair —& squabby figure—the very image of some of the plainer she peasantry. She ought to have been darkly interesting. If I may judge of German gratitude she gave her preserver a lock of tow, and advised her father to go on with his lawsuit. This sounds splenetic, but we have some right to be angry. But we are going to be politic too. I have played the part I promised in Dilke's letter as a *scold*. After on the very subject in the morning, I found that Gradle had walked off into the street or more probably on the cold banks of the Rhine (where her sweetheart works) with Tom, Junior, scarcely out of the measles, & nothing more on his back or head than he wears in the house. So I gave a good John Bull lecture, with a chorus of a word that rhymes with *lamb* but doesn't *reason* with it—& frightened her well. Thank God, Tom's as well as ever—he does not seem to have got over the measles but to have jumped over them—he is a rare strong hearty fellow worthy of his Godfather. But I must tell you of Joseph the Carpenter. He came innocently to see Gradle at the street door every night, and as that is the custom here we couldn't object—but when the weather grew colder he got into the kitchen & we couldn't get him out again. Gradle *would not* understand he was unwelcome. So he was there morn, noon, & evening—of course "not for nothing" & a *very large* hare we had one day *wouldn't* hash the next—I was thinking of translating my English into cuffing & kicking when Rampone[14] came & we made him scold for us—& she promised & gave up Joseph in all appearance. But it is only in the house. The children go to meet him, & she makes errands—& wilfully forgets half her commissions that she may go out again—& what is worse we begin to doubt she *sells*, in buying for us. 'Tis such a conspiracy against the English we could never have found it out but for Franck—'tis like free-masonry. They have double lists, double bills of fare at the inns &c, &c. And they never can mistake you however you may speak German. As an instance Franck got for us (as if for himself, & he passes for a German by name & speaks it perfectly & wears the uniform) a printed list of all articles with the prices, from one of the most respectable houses in Coblenz. They were so deep they asked him "where they should send it"—but he was not to be had & called again for it—& accordingly we find what we had paid 15 pence for is by rights only 10 & so on. But such is the system from the highest to the lowest we could not have found it out but for Franck. So we are meditating a domestic revolution or rather coup d'etat—to change lodging servant & all at once & begin de novo. I must do Rampone[15] the justice to say he has helped fairly to undeceive us—and as he has married a German & has to make shifts he is au fait— It is really disgusting. We were told direct solemn lies, as to the rent our predecessors paid for our lodgings—& I feel sure had I applied to them to know (such is the system) they would have confirmed the falsehood. It is hardly possible to conceive it—& we are very indignant. I am making enquiries & collecting *documents* to establish facts, which I mean some day to treat them with. My Doc-

[14] See p. 32.
[15] See p. 41.

tor for example in his bill has chosen to dub me *Sir* Thomas Hood—it is his own handwriting—he knows me well, what I am, has read Eugene Aram—& only fancies a *Knight's* vanity may lead him to overlook an overcharge. He does not know that I would not give a dollar to be Knight in reality—no offence to *Sir* Charles Dilke.[16] I could almost forgive him for one thing—he knew our dear Doctor Seoane[17] by *reputation*. It gave us sincere pleasure to be remembered by him—as Dilke elegantly says he is "a good anti emetic to take to heart against being sick of human nature." I wish the Queen may fall in love with him. Pray say everything kind for us when you write—I do wish I could send him a book. Tis piteous to think we may not meet again but in heaven—that is if Doctors and punsters go to heaven.—& yet tis not more unlikely that I *may* be [in?] Spain than that Green[18] *might* have been. Who knows after last year's whirl! We may all meet *done brown* in Mexico!—The Lindos[19] are in fortune's round about too. She forgot part of her commission so we had a postscript packet—containing the favour of your two packs of English cards—which Dr. Beckmann pulled a frightful face at, & informed us that the penalty was only £15 upon each! As we are on very friendly terms with de Franck we

[16] Dilke was not a Knight and was against titles on principle, so this is a mere pleasantry. His son, however, later, in 1861, accepted (against his father's advice) a baronetcy, awarded for his work on the Great Exhibition, of which he was one of the five Royal Commissioners.

[17] Dr. Mateo Seoane, a Spanish medical man of repute, was a close friend of Dilke and a reviewer of Spanish books for the *Athenaeum*.

[18] Probably Jane Hood's brother-in-law, husband of Marian Reynolds. There is no clue to the reference to Spain. Perhaps Green boasted of having been there. Hood would be inclined to distrust him. (See p. 25.)

[19] Unidentified.

have given him, (handsomels) [20] one of the packs & half the risk—so pray (with our best thanks)—send no more—it is playing "rayther eye." As for the newspapers I was luxuriating in, he says the Germans must not have them "at all, at all."

The said new[?] Doctor informs me he is going to London in the summer—of course I shall *not* give him a letter of introduction to you—but I shall insidiously give him a recommendation to seek the Westminster Medical Conversazione where I hope they will give him a *physicker*. Jane, who is writing to Mrs. Elliot, has just read to me a bit I must quote. She says I am so on the high ropes as to the impositions on the English, I shall be "seen at the arrival of every steamboat like a Bow Street officer at a mob calling out 'Gentlemen take care of your pockets.'" It is not bad for *her*—is it? Being confined to my conversation she grows funny. In the meantime we get from the library a "monthly Magazine" printed at Leipsic—extraited *wholly* from English authors & what is worse not the best of them—(such people as write in the Keepsake) [21]—but from a memoir at the end, of R. Ackermann, I have found that the English people & government gave the distressed Germans 1.333.333/10. dollars—which same I do roll up into a monstrous great choke-spear, to put at a set off to the anti-English tariff. However there are some spots at Wiesbaden & the Radzwil's & a few more where the English are the rage—& the Germans *rage* at it, they say, in proportion.

[20] Perhaps a manufactured word made from "handsel" and "handsome." A handsome handsel (gift)? Hood is capable of such forced word play.

[21] The *Keepsake*, an annual edited by the Hon. Mrs. Norton, like most of the *genre* was made up largely of poems and stories by literary hacks.

Mind—poke it well into Dilke, about Bettine [22]—when you want to plague him—whoever wrote that review had got up on a high german metaphysical horse—but I trust I have shown up *the lady on the pillion*. Seriously I am dead sick of the people hereabout—& not without cause—but I love the *country* & cannot forgive them for not being in *keeping*. So you must think of us as very comfortable and happy & reconciled—with a wholesome vent for carrying off our spleen. After all the gospel & the epistle, & the collect & the litany gone before, my amen is God bless us all & huzza for the New Year! It's unlucky for *huz* as the Scotch say, that this present Lent there is for the first time doubt of a *Carnival* which would be a novelty for *hus*. Good & bad customs seem going equally out of use: besides it spoils a good joke. I thought of going [huzy?] all over with "good 4 groshen pieces"—as a representative of the Athenaeum— Perhaps I *may* go, with Tom Junior pickaback bare legged & bareheaded—as a representative of "the English disease," alias rickets.[23] In spite of the uncertainty—this affair occupies all heads at present. I will tell you all I know. Jane in a cottage bonnet with a slice of brown bread in one hand & a German sausage in the other is to go as *Content*. Gradle carrying Tom is to represent Peace nursing Innocence—& innocence is to wear a tartan kilt to show that his legs are straight. Fanny in a pink frock, orange handkerchief sky blue apron & lilac bonnet her two tails tied with pea green, & scarlet shoes, is to represent simplicity— But farewell to fancies—I have subjects in realities.

One blow is struck of our coup d'état! It is the first ordonnance. Gradle has had warning! Prepare for a domestic revolution like that of Stoke Poges! As usual there is

[22] See pp. 44-46.
[23] See p. 43.

plenty of farce in it. This morning (Sunday 31st) Gradle went to mass before breakfast—after which we received thro Fanny our Dragoman, a desire from the Priest that Gradle should come to church. This was evidently a fictitious message or else a very impertinent one from his reverence. We took no notice—the understanding being Gradle is to go every other Sunday, *if convenient*, & when we have been able we have sent her *out of turn*. Church time comes —& behold *Joseph*—not of Arimathea tho a carpenter. As a charity, as it was represented, I gave him *some two months ago* a black coat (No. 3) & wondered what he had done with it—when today out he comes, with a new velvet collar put to my old coat—instead of his prussian cap a new *round hat* (I wear an old one) minus his constant pipe,—in fact a perfect parody of "the English gentleman", only, if anything a little more stylish. This we only laughed at.—Having letters to write to England & the day being fine Gradle was told to take the children a walk, & the route indicated. She made no objection but dressed in her best, & set forth up Nail Street. However, when she thought I was hard at work at easy writing & Jane boggling at sentimentals, she retraced her steps, & (passing the house, with her *brazen* censer of incense) marched the children off to St. Castor's. I chanced to see it—but in spite of St. Castor & the Priest, Fanny did not choose to be diddled out of her walk and remonstrated with all her German might in the Vicar's presence—whereupon Gradle brought my little Protestants home again under a pretense that it rained. Only think of this! To have Bunyan's Holy War in your own house—and I am of course Diabolus! Jane is Mrs. Martin Luther! You know how I always stuck up for Church of England & only knew the Vicar of Wanstead of all its people—the father of the Albigensian *Gilly*—not a highland gilly. Thereupon I—

79

spit her spite. She told Fanny "she didn't like Jane—she'd leave her—she was ill treated &c."—which Fanny reported not forgetting a guttural. Then in the bedroom, Fanny brought *indirect* messages that "she needn't go out with G. again—not to stay in the room &c."—whereupon Jane went in & flared up English & German chopped up together like a lobster salad. I'm sorry to say again I did not hear it. However Franck came & hearing the case & taking Fanny's evidence, *in German,*—& moreover knowing we meant to give her warning, instead of any explanation he only said to her in his military style (tho it went against the Calendar) "On the first of *February*—March!!!" I am afraid this abrupt word of command of Franck's will make Jane ill of a great deal of suppressed motley eloquence. Perhaps she will vent it on me. As for Gradle—this very instant the doorbell sounds—& as if it were a race Jane exclaims "she's off!"—A moment, & Joseph will know it—& all the rest of the Holy Family—(Of course there is one). But do not grieve for us—we shall get a better and a cheaper by ⅓. The English, however, will be in worse odour. I hope she won't kill De Franck. Jane fears she will poison Fanny—& doubtless will look her over every night for blue spots as she would for flea-bites. I feel a little burning in my own throat. In case I should never be able to address you again, believe me my dear Mrs. Dilke

Yours ever in the next world very truly

Thos. Hood.

[Postscript written crosswise in red ink on first & second pages]

I think Dilke does not care to read crossed letters—& thus we may keep our correspondence to ourselves. You will *find* that I have written at very great length—indeed like a

Boa Constrictor determined to swallow up all your leisure. But be comforted. It will be some time before you have from me even a little wiper again—I have other fish to fry if I may say so where there are frying pans but no fish— As to health Tom is a giant—I am as well as ever I was & Jane no worse—Fanny is delicate but we hope to mend her—Our spirits are good.—Yesterday Jane made some potted beef—& I almost choked her and De Franck by insisting that she had *chewed* it—& as she had a face ache & was holding her jaw at the time it seemed to be a certainty. —You see we can cook a little without much more apparatus than God has given us. Moreover she contrived to make a mince pie on a large scale—only as it was a novelty the Baker stole half its *inside*. So if you come out *you* need not live a fortnight on baked potatoes as you did at Paris— Save up your pin money and come—we shall make much of you and little of Dilke—& there you will both be of a size— There is a doubt whether the review will be at Cologne or here but we shall have early intelligence— [24]

The first steamboat from Rotterdam is expected here to-night—it feels very pleasant as repairing a broken link with England—I have no more news—I would not trust the Editor with my reminiscences—but pray give our kind regards to Chorley, Taylor, Holmes,[25] & all who ask of us— As for yourselves, we do hope to see you—but till then give us credit for all kind feelings & good wishes— Do not forget Wentworth, though he should be keeping term or Wil-

[24] The great military review took place at Coblenz in September, 1836, while the Dilkes were visiting the Hoods. (See *Memorials,* I, 197-201.)

[25] Henry Chorley was Dilke's right-hand man on the *Athenaeum* and later a music critic of some note. W. Cooke Taylor was also one of Dilke's reviewers. James Holmes was the printer of the *Athenaeum* and owned a quarter interest in the periodical.

liam [26] tho he should be with you— Jane sends her love &
will write when my letter has *evaporated*— She accuses me
of forestalling her news—as Dilke complained of you. But
more will turn up—Fanny desires her love & an everlasting
German Kiss to her Godmama

Your[s] ag[a]in

T. H.

[The Party]

[no date] [Nov., 1841, or 1842?]
My dear Mrs. Dilke. I am very glad to hear that you think
the party went off so well. Of course next day we were
rather snoozy gapey & indolent & like the wild Beasts after
Barthemy Fair, very tame indeed. Tom excepted who
ought to have been dozey but was as brisk as a bee. So
much for youth. I lay in bed very late like Watt's Sluggard
& made my reflections on the guests—What good spirits
you were in & how frisky the Editor [1] was—with a deal of
dance left in him when he went. Then that very popular
Punch!! for which every body must have been better—&
how well your boy waited—but I beg pardon for you were
described below stairs as "the lady with the Page" (I'd
make Dilke indulge me in a double number [2] of such
pages). And all the servants lauded him so that our boy
grew jealous & said "you'd better lap him up in gold
paper"—Another young lady, who had no page, was not
so happily described as *the lady who tumbled* up stairs.

[26] Unidentified, though probably some relative of Dilke. Wentworth was Dilke's only son.

[1] Dilke.

[2] Dilke, as editor of the *Athenaeum*, gave his readers a great many
"double numbers" with twice the ordinary number of pages.

Then they had never heard such singing—Jane (the servant) thought herself I suspect within sound of the Angelic quire—for she is of a decidedly pious turn. Marian's [3] voice made quite a sensation—everybody was asking me about her—& then Mr. Hook [4] was so taken with your singing he said it was one of the best ballad voices he had ever heard. So I think you may come next time as the Countess of Essex—only don't come from Antwerp or you won't come at all—like the Countess de Melfort, who was *missed* thro *fog*. However, the thing seemed really to go off well & all *parties* to be pleased—and it will be well if with Colburn's puffing propensity his Editor's [party?] does not get into the Post.[5] But now comes a preciously short month & I must work double tides—that Xmas revelries may not be cut short. That's the way we Editors must go from gay to grave from lively to severe.—i.e. from cheerful guests to dull contributors, from a Bayle Farm Frîte to Squampash Flats.

I shall tell you *no more* that something may be left to

[3] Probably Hood's sister-in-law, Marian Reynolds Green. (See p. 15 ff.) Apparently the quarrel of 1835 had been forgotten or forgiven.

[4] This is probably not Theodore Hook, novelist and editor of the *New Monthly Magazine* before Hood, for the indication of the letter is that Hood was editor at the time of writing and he took that job on the death of Hook in August, 1841. The greater probability is that it refers to the Mr. Hook mentioned in the *Memorials* (II, 83) as Hood's lawyer in the case against Baily.

[5] Henry Colburn was the chief publisher in London of the so-called "novels of fashion" and memoirs of high society. He was notorious for inspiring favorable reviews of his books in his own periodicals, of which the *New Monthly Magazine*, then edited by Hood, was one. Hood would have nothing to do with this "trade criticism" and soon left his editorial post. The reference here is to Colburn's practice of puffing his authors and editors by inserting paid or "stimulated" social gossip about them in the newspapers.

talk over when we see you—which however is impossible thro so much fog.—not to mention streets, parks, &c. hardly more solid.—

I hope you all got home safe & that Mrs. Wentworth was no worse for the weather. I meant to go out today but am afraid of losing myself—& don't like to be my own link boy.—

N.B. Your note just arrived which I leave Jane to answer having to write a little Ode to whist—a sonnet on hearing a lady sing— Stanzas on witnessing a quadrille—& Punch, a reverie. I am

My dear Mrs. D.

Yours very truly
Thos. Hood.

["Si Sick Omnes"]

17 Elm Tree Road [1842?]

My dear Mrs. Dilke.

As Jane has written so awkwardly, for a correspondent, I mean to try my luck, and to ensure our letters not crossing I shall return you your own with my comments in a different ink.[1]

"Dilke has been very ill the last four or five days—*Yes, with the Athenaeum up to Friday*—not able to get out of his bed—*no, he was always an inveterate you know what*—but yesterday there was a great change for the better—*& whoever laid the first stone of the Great 'Change Dilke no doubt was at the feast*—and today is so fine he has gone out for a little drive *he ought to have walked*—and as that is the

---

[1] Hood's comments are here given in italics. In the manuscript they were in red ink.

case—*a very mild one,*—I think I may venture to ask you and Hood *nothing venture nothing have*—& one or two more to join us in a family dinner on the 18th—Wentworth's Birthday—*Wentworth—what, a family dinner for one child!* —a ¼ before 6—*nonsense—he's* 7 *if he's a day* [2]—do come if you can—*what an if!* as we really want to see you—*a bit of ground bait to get us to bite!*

Are you going to Colburn's on Tuesday? *Of course—it would be a day after the fair on Wednesday.* We have had an invitation to meet Lady Morgan [3] & a few literary friends—*and a blue Hare?* but Dilke of course is too unwell —*si sick omnes!!!*

I want to get a walk—*Walker!* that I know you will excuse my saying more than my kind love to you all &

Believe me yours ever

M. D.

(*No God bless—think it's a forgery*)

S.P. Let me hear from you soon—*Who hinders you?*

Yours ever truly

Thos. Hood.

P.S. Many thanks for the orders—We'll be sure to come—but mind & keep places for us—two—*dress circle—first row.*

P.P.S. *The last paragraph is in the wrong ink which ought to have been red. I am not accustomed to be read in M.S. but in print.*

Jane would add her hand but from haste only puts her finger.

[finger print]

---

[2] Wentworth was born in 1810 and so was about 32 when this was written.

[3] Lady Morgan (Sydney Owenson), the author of *The Wild Irish Girl* and other popular novels as well as travel books, was a close friend of the Dilkes and a frequent reviewer for the *Athenaeum*.

[Shoberl and Colburn]

Wednesday [no other date] [1843?]

Dear Dilke

Moxon [1] was here today & says Lord W. Lennox [2] came to him about a novel—that he said *he only gave a sort of outline & heads of chapters & others filled them up.* I have no doubt after the exposé he will declare the true writer— I have strong suspicions of Shoberl [3] being the man.

He wrote to me decidedly as from Lord L.—ending with a proposal to call on me to know whether I was willing to comply *"with Lord L's request."* Lord Lenox [sic] wrote to me that he did not authorize the application tho he had named me as the person he should prefer to write a preface —but that Shoberl should have applied as from Colburn.[4] I wrote to ask Shoberl if he was authorized by Colburn & he wrote that he was <u>not</u> but had *"applied of his own accord!"*

I have not seen the book yet—& have said nothing at Colburn's of the discovery—but from the above have concluded that Shoberl was the true plagiarist,[5] wanted to entrap me into an apparent sanction of the work.

[1] Edward Moxon. (See p. 59.)

[2] Lord William Pitt Lennox, sportsman, dandy, and miscellaneous writer, had at one time been aide-de-camp to the Duke of Wellington. He was the original of the Lord Prima Donna in Disraeli's novel of high society *Vivian Grey*. He wrote a number of feeble novels, by what method is suggested here. The novel in question, as indicated in the following letter, was *The Tuft Hunter* (1843).

[3] Frederic Shoberl was co-founder with Henry Colburn and chief sub-editor of the *New Monthly Magazine*. While Hood was editor, Shoberl evidently wrote many of the puffing reviews for the magazine for his master Colburn without consulting Hood. (See p. 83.)

[4] See p. 83.

[5] Further evidence is given in the following letter.

Yesterday morning I swore my affidavit in the common pleas, & shall have news tonight how the other party meet it,—[6] we are going to a [second sheet torn off]

[The Tuft Hunter]

Thursday [no other date] [1843?]

Dear Dilke.

The Tuft Hunter [1] appears to be one of the grossest cases possible. I have only seen the 1st. Vol. from a Library—& stumbled on passages taken from Sir W. Scott. Compare pages 243-244-245, 248 with St. Ronan's Well—pages 3-4-5-6-13—(Vol. 34 of Tusher's Edition of the Novels).

I have just received a note from Shoberl in reference to his former ones—he marks it "Confidential" which I interpret "No word of this to Mr. Colburn." He encloses a letter from Lord L. to him (Shoberl) dated 18 Jany—which confirms Lord L's to me viz—that the *suggestion* about me & a preface was to be made to Colburn. Shoberl did *not* consult Colburn but comes to me as with a direct request from Lord L. This I think convicts S. of the Authorship by his personal interest in the scheme. We passed your end of Grosvenor Place this morning—but as it was between 4 & 5 we did not drop in.

[6] A reference to Hood's legal proceedings against his former publisher, A. H. Baily. (See Introduction, p. 11, and p. 52.)

[1] See previous letter and notes.

["Fun Out of Colburn"]

[no date] [probably late Feb., 1843]

Dear Dilke

You have done it very well—the thing shows itself up, or you might have been perhaps severer upon it— [1] Lord L. is a fool, but the other is a thorough rogue, & double traitor,—the *system* deserves denouncing—however I have thundered a bit at the attempt to connect me with it—& am having my fun out of Colburn. Last night, in a sort of scheme of the contents of the Magazine [2] I quietly inserted my own first article on the list as "The Literary Daw"— they will be in a regular stew about it—& I mean to say if he does not like it, I can use it elsewhere.

Also as Lord L. has said the thing was done by one of Colburn's "literary friends" & he has admitted it,—I have urged on him the propriety of giving up the man, & not leaving the slur amongst the Authors & Authoresses of his acquaintance, going thro the list—beginning with Lord Londonderry—Morgans, Bulwer, H. Smith, Lady Blessington, &c, &c., &c. And as he did not like my fixing it on his Clerk, I have guessed again, from the ignorance of the work, borrowing half sentences even, that it must *be the porter!*

In the meantime as the fellow gets off scot free & I have not had the slightest [next page torn off]

[1] See the beautifully satirical review of *The Tuft Hunter* in the *Athenaeum*, February 25, 1843, pp. 178-179. The review, probably by Dilke, shows that the author of the book, whether Lennox or Shoberl, was guilty of gross plagiarism, having stolen whole paragraphs not only from Sir Walter Scott but also from Hood's *Tylney Hall.*

[2] The *New Monthly Magazine*. (See p. 86.)

Short Letters and Fragments

[Passport]

[1835?] [1]

My dear Dilke

I shall be later than 6.—½ past say,—I have got my pass-port & have left it at the Prussian to get backed,—if the sec^y. should be there before 6. If not I must take it as it is. Not to be idle I wrote to my neighbor the Duke,[2] & he has sent me a very handsome note, with a billet in French to show in a difficulty, giving me a good character & as enjoying his "connoissance" & esteem.

Yours ever truly

Thos.

address: C. W. Dilke, Esqre
Clarence Club
12 Waterloo Place.

[1] The internal evidence indicates that this letter was probably written in April, 1835, just before Hood left for Coblenz.
[2] Probably the Duke of Devonshire for whom Hood had written some punning book titles to go on the Duke's library door. (See *Memorials*, I, 30 ff.)

[Ode for the *Athenaeum*]

[Fragment of letter addressed to:]
C. W. Dilke (Junr) Esqre
Athenaeum Office
Catherine Street
Strand
[post stamp:] Ostend 29 Oct., 1837

As for an Ode for the Ath. it must depend on the inspiration. If you have it at all, it shall be in good time—but I am very busy on the Comic, & today, at least, feel not in the best order for writing. Mrs. Hood desires her kind regards with thou

Affectionately Dear Wentworth
[signature torn out]

[Contributions to *Athenaeum*]

[fragment of letter] [French post mark—probably from Ostend] [Winter, 1837, 38, or 39?]

My dear Dilke.

I fear the bit on the other side is not good for anything—as I am not at all in writing trim. Your letter found me yesterday with my head quite muddled with pain. I had struggled well with the very severe frost but the suddenness of the thaws upset me. I shall be well after a night's rest, as I barely winked till this morning. This ought to reach on Friday morning—but our mails have been very irregular through the blockade of ice. I Murphy'd this weather when I was at Blackheath. I am quite awake to the importance of something of *current* interest for the 2 next Nos. & in fact have been studying it. I shall well consider your suggestions which look likely ones. I will take care to be on time. [rest torn out]

[Influenza]

[1840 or after?]
Fenchurch Street [1]

My dear Dilke.

Yours, in Times for the Barnes.—[2] Verbum Sap.

By dint of turning a Common boatman, I have got rid of the dress of the Influenza—at the expense of the skin of my nose,—my left temple—& cheek bone.

I shall not say more or I shall not be conversible at your dinner.

My love to the Dilkes, & as Elliston [3] used to say whether "in the House or out of the House."

[signature torn out]

["Damn Baily"]

[Fragment]   [1840 or after?]

My dear Dilke.—damn Baily.[4]

The enclosed with very many thanks.

[1] Fenchurch Street was the business address of John Wright. (See p. 27.)

[2] The reference here is not clear. Barnes was editor of the *Times*.

[3] Robert William Elliston, actor and one time manager of Drury Lane Theatre.

[4] Probably written while Hood was involved in the lawsuit with his former publisher, A. H. Baily. (See p. 87.)

[Day and Hughes]

17 Elm Tree Road [1841 or after?]
Monday

Dear Dilke,

The note we want is one that Day & Hughes wrote to you, to say they thought it as well to state the reason for declining your proposal was that the stock was attached.[1]

Mrs. Dilke sent me a copy of the note but without the date—it must have been I think in *July*, 1840.

I am

Dear Dilke.

[signature torn out]

C.W. Dilke Esquire.

["Amusing Paragraphs"]

[1842 or 1843?]

From my bed room where I am nursing myself for a spasmodic attack of the lungs.—sharpish, but I am getting all right.

My dear Dilke.

Happening the other day to pick up an odd Vol. of an old book amongst some waste paper, I have extracted & enclose a few amusing paragraphs which may help to make up with, in your column of odds & ends.—If you like them I have noted a few more for extract.

[1] The reference probably is to the attachment of the stock of Hood's works in the hands of A. H. Baily by a creditor of Hood. (See Hood's letter to the *Athenaeum*, Oct. 17, 1840, p. 829.) Perhaps Dilke had tried to sell the stock for Hood to Day and Hughes.

I have just got your note & am much pleased that you liked the articles.[1] Thanks for the No. which reads capitally.—I hope Lection [?] has a great increase of business.—I am looking out for another little book to do but send off these to be with you early.

I will write to the Secy & shall like to be on the Committee [2]—if it be but necessary to attend occasionally—

With joint kind regards to you, I am

My dear Dilke

[signature torn out]

[The Gig and the Pig]

[Fragment—no clue to date]

I have had a spill out of my gig & have hurt my hand but I shall be able to cut my own victuals. Can I bring anything acceptable with me—a Small Porker that might pass

---

[1] Possibly Hood's last two articles on "Copyright and Copywrong," published in the *Athenaeum* in 1842.

[2] The reference may be to a committee of a society for the defense of copyright, a subject in which both Dilke and Dickens were interested. Hood had proposed such a society in 1842 in a letter to Dickens published in the *Memorials* (II, 143). In another letter to Dickens in 1843 Hood wrote: "As to the society they knew that you & I and Dilke should pull together, in the Committee. However I can act as a Free Lance—help the society if I see fit, & if not, like an Irish Partisan I'll co-operate against it. In the mean time it seems to me that they have declared for the Integrity with a sneaking kindness towards the *Tegg*-rity of Literary Property." [MS letter in Huntington Library.]

The reference in the last sentence of this quotation is to Thomas Tegg, who made a fortune in cheap reprints and abridgments of popular works, and because of the looseness of the copyright laws paid nothing to the authors whose works he reprinted. He was caricatured as Twigg, a pirating bookseller, in Hood's *Tylney Hall* and was mentioned by Carlyle in his plea for the Copyright Bill.

for a roast, sucking-pig, if set before the bulk of Dilke Senr—?—or a deformed cucumber—or two new laid eggs— or a couple of chickens as big as blackbirds or a few young ducks?

Hood

Miscellanies—Poetry and Prose

[Drinking Song]

Let others of Dorchester quaff at their pleasure [1]
Or honour old men with their special regard
We *imbibe* (drink) Adam's ale,—& can get it pool measure,[2]
Or quaff heavy wet[?] from the butt in the yard!
   Then hey for a bucket.
Should fortune diminish our cash's sum total,
Deranging our wits & our private affairs,
Tho some in such cares would fly to the bottle
There's nothing like water for drowning our cares—
   Then hey for a bucket.
In wine let a lover remember his jewel
And pledge her in bumpers fill'd brimming & oft,
But we can distinguish the kind from the cruel
And *pledge* (toast) them in water—the hard or the soft
   Then hey!
Some, crossed in their passion can *never o'erlook* (ne'er
 overlook) it,

[1] This is apparently a first draft of a poem published in Hood's
Comic Annual for 1837 with the title: "Drinking Song, by a member
of a Temperance Society, as sung by Mr. Spring at Waterman's
Hall." Before publication three stanzas not included here were
added, the order of the stanzas was considerably changed, and the
wording of some lines was altered.
[2] Here and in the following miscellanies and fragments italics indi-
cate words crossed out by Hood in the manuscript, while the sub-
stitutions are given in parentheses.

But take to a pistol, a razor—or beam,
Whilst the temperate swains, are enabled to brook it
All along by the side of a pastoral stream!
(By help of a *sweet purling* little meandering stream!)
                    Then hey!
Let topers of grape juice exultingly vapour,
But let us just mention a word to the elves
We water roads, horses, silks, ribbons, bank paper,
Plants, poets & muses & why not ourselves?
                    Then hey—&c & But
Some flatter gin, brandy & rum for their merits
Grog punch & what not *to* (that) enliven their *feasts* (**a**
        feast);
True water may give us
Tis true (that) they *enliven* (stir up) the animal spirits,—
But may not the animal turn to a beast.

The vintage they cry—think of Spain's & of France's
Their *reels the* (peasant's) boleros fandangos & jumps,
But water's the spring of all civilized Dances,
We go to a ball not in bottles but pumps
                    Then hey!
Then Man in the Ark, that *preserved the whole* (continued
        our) species
He did it on water—& not upon wine
We all know *what* the figure more sad than facetious
We make after tasting the juice of the *wines* (vine)!

Come fill up your pails [poem ends here in manuscript]

[Civil War]

There is perhaps nothing more deplorable in the world than the barbarism of what is called Civil War—an epithet evidently applied ironically and implying only the sort of civility that belongs to other domestic feuds when "my Duck" is equivalent to "my Devil." It is however a question worthy of the 19th Century whether civil war might not be literally civilized & imbued with even a courteous spirit. Otherwise it is a misnomer that repudiates the notion of an Urban Gerard without urbanity. *Why should not Dragoons show good breeding.* A really civil General [breaks off here]

["Ivy Crowned Bacchus"]

There's dilke—from devotion to port & to Sherry,[1]
Has, got, at Coblenz in a *very* (thorough) wrong box,—
Who thought, at the vintage to be very merry,
And *standing* (treading) in Rhenish quite up to his Locks
    [or Socks?],—
Then, let them crown Bacchus, *with ivy*, (exult in a flash &
    a jorum,) jorum
As ivy crown'd Bacchus—   *& stagger to bed,*
A water cress wreath
And greenish with cress as through Myddelton's head,—
Whilst others (Then let them) exult in a bottle or jorum,
An ivy crown'd Bacchus so bloated & red.
Let's drink the "New River"—& place with decorum
A water cress wreath on Huggle Myddelton's head!

[1] Possibly written while the Dilkes were visiting the Hoods at Coblenz in September, 1836.

["I Must Have Meat"]

But me—I really can't obey the censors
    I must have meat
    Some twice a day to eat
The <u>coats</u> of my stomach are not <u>spencers</u> plate-armour.[2]

[Generosity Towards Foreigners]

Sir.

I had heard so high a character abroad of the hospitality & of the generosity of the English Nation towards Foreigners—the more foreign the more kind—that I cannot express the disappointment I have felt as a stranger, at my reception on her shores.—I could mention at least 17 cases where I have been ill treated—in London alone—to say nothing of Shields Mudselburgh &c.

        I always fed well even from the lap
          and never left my pap.

   The coats
        ration-   drum

[Cholera and Hunger]

Sir.

I have read in one of the reports of Cholera, that it generally attacks the hungry—those who have gone long without eating—in short that the worst cases are empty cases. (I mean no offense to Mr. Perceval—but) Would not a

[2] Underscored in the manuscript.

general feed—be better than a general fast—Had we not better be stuff'd alive,

hold fast!

Mr Spencer—
Thou dispenser   retrencher of the trencher
With eating & with drinking—   —3d.
Thou hast set me on much serious thing—   hearse—
I think that mutton piety were better
Fresh water'd cods & eggs are bad for cholera
                              (& end) Hunger!—
My fast-run race
     stuffing—may be stuff & nonsense.
Hast thou not heard for want of *butchering*
Of butchering and cheesemongery
The most have died in Hungary—   the Want—is wanton
My health is very very far from strong
    My appetite in fact is of that sort.
I really can't go long
    So short!—& chafe   die wantons for want
  but above   rubbings
One must *from* (for) safety get into the chafe
    a sort
Of long "Tom Copper" singing out hold fast.
                         Let us no fast day—but a
                         fast night keep
                         I mean Sir fast-asleep

[Conundrums]

Why are people apt to get deaf as they grow old?—Because
they wax in years.

What would be the best Xtian name for the gin drinking
multitude?—Maxy-million.

What is the shape of the teacups &c. when they are cleared
away?—A tea-tray-gone.

What is the coldest month of the year? January is cold,
but Febber-wery!

What is a blunderbuss?—Getting into the wrong omnibus.

When is a man twice an Ass?—When he's ass-ass-inated.

What is a mongrel?—An animal that starts for two races
& is not placed in either.

What is the worst sort of Magpie?—A kag-mag pie.

TRANSLATION

Aurum pot-a-bile. Gold biles the pot.

When is Mohammed of Brighton an Imitator?—When he is
going to sham-poo Hill.

Why is a boy that runs away from school like a pismire?—
Because he's a true-ant.

EPIGRAM

So steam that does so many turns
Is brought to drive the coach at last,
Well hast thou sung O Robert Burns,
That "Life is but a Kittle cast"!

HOOD

Chronological Table

OF THE PRINCIPAL EVENTS IN THE LIFE OF THOMAS HOOD [1]

1799—Born May 23, at 31 Poultry, London. Father a publisher.

1811—Father died. Family living at Lower Street, Islington.

c. 1813—Briefly apprenticed as a clerk.

c. 1814—Took up engraving.

1815—In the autumn went to Dundee on a visit to relatives for his health's sake.

1816—Dundee. Probably wrote some poetry and made first contributions (unidentified) to local periodicals.

1817—Dundee. Returned to London in the autumn. Probably apprenticed as engraver.

1818-1820—Probably busy as engraver, and doing some writing.

1821—In the summer became sub-editor of the *London Magazine* and a frequent contributor, running for it a department called "The Lion's Head." Close friendship with John Hamilton Reynolds (1794-1852).[2] Possibly also met Charles Wentworth Dilke (1789-1864) [But see Introduction, p. 6]

[1] Based partly on the table prepared by Walter Jerrold for the Oxford Edition of Hood's poems.

[2] For evidence concerning the birth dates of John and Jane Reynolds see George L. Marsh's "New Data on Keats's Friend Reynolds," *Modern Philology*, Vol. XXV, Feb., 1928, pp. 320-321.

1822—In August *Gil Blas* (dramatization by Hood and Reynolds) produced at the English Opera House. In the autumn became engaged to Jane Reynolds (1793?-1846).[2] Probably met Lamb in early months of this year.

c. 1823—Ceased to sub-edit the *London Magazine*.

1825—Hood's "Hogarthian" plate, *The Progress of Cant* (praised by Lamb, now a warm friend of Hood), and his and Reynolds's *Odes and Addresses to Great People* published. Married Jane Reynolds, May 5. At 2 Robert St., Adelphi, London.

1826—*Whims and Oddities*, first series (first book written and illustrated by Hood himself). Appointed dramatic critic of the *Atlas*.

1827—First daughter born and died in May; occasion for Lamb's poem "On an Infant Dying as soon as Born." *Whims and Oddities*, second series. *Plea of the Midsummer Fairies and other Poems. National Tales* (published by Harrison Ainsworth).

1828—At Brighton after severe attack of rheumatic fever.

1829—Rose Cottage, Winchmore Hill (not far from Enfield where Lamb lived). Edited the *Gem*, an annual, and contributed to it "The Dream of Eugene Aram." Published *The Epping Hunt*.

1830—Daughter, Frances Freeling, born (exact date not known—died 1878). *Comic Annual* begun (published late in 1829 by Hurst, Chance & Company). Part proprietor with Dilke and Reynolds of the *Athenaeum*.

1831—*Dream of Eugene Aram* published separately. *Comic Annual* published by Charles Tilt. Reynolds, and prob-

[2] For evidence concerning the birth dates of John and Jane Reynolds see George L. Marsh's "New Data on Keats's Friend Reynolds," *Modern Philology*, Vol. XXV, Feb., 1928, pp. 320-321.

ably Hood, sold interest in *Athenaeum* to Dilke but continued to contribute.

1832—Removed to Lake House, Wanstead.

1834—Published *Tylney Hall*. In the autumn changed publishers from Charles Tilt to A. H. Baily. Suffered financial loss through the failure of a (publishing?) firm.

1835—Only son, Tom, born January 19 (died 1874). Jane Hood seriously ill. Dr. Elliot, who attended Mrs. Hood, became close family friend. Went to Coblenz in March; joined by family in April (372 Castor Hof). Frequent illnesses.

1836—Coblenz (752 Alten Graben, from June). Visited by Dilkes in September. Trip with Lieutenant De Franck's regiment as far as Berlin (October-November).

1837—Removed to Ostend, June (39, Rue Longue). Visited by Wright and Dilkes in autumn.

1838—Ostend. Began monthly publication of *Hood's Own*, made up from *Comic Annuals* with additions. Suffering from poor health, visited London for three weeks to consult Dr. Elliot, stayed with the Dilkes. Last *Comic Annual* (for 1839—published late in 1838).

1839—Ostend (La Rhétorique, Rue St. François). *Hood's Own* published as volume. Continued illnesses.

1840—Ostend. *Up the Rhine* (actually appeared before Christmas, 1839), last work of Hood published by A. H. Baily, who, Hood felt, had been unfair in business dealings. Started legal action against Baily. Visited Dilke in January, and Dr. Elliot in April. Ill for several weeks at Dr. Elliot's home. The Hoods returned permanently to England in August (2 Union Street, High Street, Camberwell).

1841—Became editor of the *New Monthly Magazine* after

the death of Theodore Hook (August). Removed to 17 Elm Tree Road, St. John's Wood (or at beginning of 1842). Friendship with Dickens.

1842—*Comic Annual* started again (from Hood's contributions to *New Monthly Magazine*).

1843—Gave up editorship of *New Monthly Magazine*, autumn. "The Song of the Shirt" published in the Christmas number of *Punch*. Removed to Devonshire Lodge, New Finchley Road, after Christmas.

1844—*Hood's Magazine*, started in January. Seriously ill for months. Civil list pension granted to Mrs. Hood in November.

1845—Died after lingering illness, May 3. Buried at Kensal Green.